I0143624

WHAT IN THE WILDERNESS IS GOING ON?

A GUIDE TO FIND YOUR WAY OUT OF THE WILDERNESS AND INTO YOUR PROMISE.

MIKE ROBINSON

WHAT IN THE WILDERNESS IS GOING ON?
A Guide To Find Your Way Out Of The
Wilderness And Into Your Promise
By Mike Robinson

ISBN: 979-8-9917173-0-4

All Rights Reserved. No part of this publication may be produced or transmitted in any form or by any means without written permission of the author. The author guarantees all contents are original and do not infringe upon the legal rights of any other person or work.

Prepared for Publication By

B|B
PUBLISHING
MAKING YOUR BOOK A REALITY

Cedar Point, NC | 843-929-8768 | info@BandBpublishingLLC.com

Scripture quotations marked NKJV are taken from the New King James Version®. Copyright © 1982 by Thomas Nelson. Used by permission. All rights reserved.

Scripture quotations marked KJV are taken from The Holy Bible, King James Version.

Scripture quotations marked NIV are taken from New International Version. THE HOLY BIBLE, NEW INTERNATIONAL VERSION®, NIV® Copyright © 1973, 1978, 1984, 2011 by Biblica, Inc.® Used by permission. All rights reserved worldwide

Scripture quotations marked NLT are taken from the Holy Bible, New Living Translation, copyright © 1996, 2004, 2015 by Tyndale House Foundation. Used by permission of Tyndale House Publishers, Inc., Carol Stream, Illinois 60188. All rights reserved.

Scripture quotations taken from the Amplified® Bible (AMPC), Copyright © 1954, 1958, 1962, 1964, 1965, 1987 by The Lockman Foundation Used by permission. lockman.org"

Scripture quotations are from The ESV® Bible (The Holy Bible, English Standard Version®), © 2001 by Crossway, a publishing ministry of Good News Publishers. Used by permission. All rights reserved.

To Contact the Author
Mike Robinson
PO Box 85
827 1st Ave.
Friendsville, MD. 21531
Email: Mike@anchorchurch.live

CONTENTS

Dedication

To my Lord and Savior Jesus Christ; who is the ultimate example of conquering the wilderness, my Heavenly Father; who watches over me and the Holy Spirit, who leads me.

Then to my wife Sandy who stood in Faith with me, fought for me in prayer, became my medical advocate and carried the weight of five people without complaint. She is a hero!

To my family and closest friends. To those amazing prayer warriors who prayed for me.

Finally to all those who are walking through the wilderness, may this be a map to help you on your providential trek through that wilderness.

MIKE ROBINSON

Endorsements

I read one to three books per month, rarely do I read a book in one setting (unless it's pretty small). Like most avid readers, I have several books open at the same time and often don't finish them all. But this one! I was captured by Mike's storytelling ability, especially how he tells the story of his own life and how he has overcome sundry trials and afflictions that would take out the person with a casual commitment to God and His Word. But then, Mike is not causally committed to the things he values in life, God, Family, Ministry, and Friends! As he mentions in the book, I have walked alongside him and his wife Sandy for over 25 years now, since 1999, and have watched him dig deeper into God with every step in the Wilderness journey he has traversed. It goes without saying that he has chosen to do what Christian author and scholar Warren Wiersbe said, "The Bumps Are What You Climb On." He has chosen to go over, around or through near death sickness, church betrayals, financial hardship, mental torment and whatever else

Satan threw his way, to discover an intimacy with God that only comes in the "furnace of affliction" where purification and circumcision takes place, resulting in a "sonship" that portrays the love between "Father and son." I am very proud to call him a spiritual son, close friend and spiritual brother. You don't get there with very many folks in your short life on earth, but the ones that have that kind of place in your heart are the real treasures of life. Please avail yourself to this faith building saga of victory through Jesus Christ and read it with your journal handy because I'm sure Holy Spirit will make some applications to your own life.

John Polis
President, Revival Fellowship International, Inc
John Polis Ministries
Faith Church Network.

"For our light affliction, which is but for a moment, is working for us a far more exceeding and eternal weight of glory" 2 Corinthians 4:17 NKJV

In the above verse The Apostle Paul shares an extremely important truth that every child of God who has aligned themselves with the Lord must embrace, accept, and understand. A primary reality of the Christian life is that there will be wilderness experiences that are not only allowed by the Lord, but on many occasions, they are even ordained by Him in our lives in order to adequately prepare us not only for the glory beyond this present age, but also for the needed brokenness, contrition, and humility needed in order for us to safely and properly experience and steward God's glory in this present age.

As I read the following manuscript written by my dear friend and longtime ministry colleague Mike Robinson entitled, "What in the Wilderness is Going On?" I was encouraged, stirred, and deeply challenged by its message and content. Not only does Mike do an amazing job describing the wilderness experienced by those who do not know Jesus, he also masterfully presents a detailed picture of what followers of Jesus experience when they enter wilderness seasons.

As you read the following pages you will experience the needed pressure within God's kingdom and eternal purposes that is utilized to produce enlargement in light of our personal growth, kingdom usage, and overall spiritual development. It is this divine pressure that allows us to become like an immovable tree (which will be further explained in this book). It is the role of some trees to simply stand while others fall under pressure, and it is this willingness and ability fueled by grace to stand that reveals a level of eternal profitability which brings God His deserved glory.

As you read you will also experience a personal journey by a man that has stood and withstood many wilderness seasons as a result of challenges to his health, his family, his finances, his calling, etc. This book is not just another work intended to educate you; its primary focus is to impact you. Therefore, Mike transparently reveals multiple levels of wilderness seasons in his own life. Beyond that, he also reveals needed practical truths that have become moorings in his own journey, family, and ministry.

Over the years I have read multiple books that focus on spiritual growth, leadership, and practical development; however, this book is clearly different from all of those. There is a message of maturity coupled within divine intimacy with Jesus that breaks through the ever-present questions about life, concerns about temporal challenges, pain that comes from ministry, etc. that reverberates from the following pages. I challenge you to read with a receptive heart and ask the Lord to speak to you and take you deeper into your walk with Him.

Lastly, I want to challenge you to see this book as a resource that you return to many times and also give to others in order to help them develop deep roots in their own lives. I am honored to fully endorse and recommend this resource and pray that its reach will go far and wide in the days ahead.

Sincerely,
Keith Collins
Generation Impact Ministries &
Impact Global Fellowship (Founder)

WHAT IN THE WILDERNESS IS GOING ON ?

There are two types of wilderness seasons. The first happens so we can find God, and the second happens so we can know God more fully. They both have a divine purpose.

The first wilderness happens to all people at some point. The outcome depends on our response to God. In this wilderness, our path in life becomes unclear or even non-existent. In the book of Ecclesiastes, the Bible makes the following statement about God and every human;

"He has made everything beautiful in its time. Also, he has put eternity into man's heart, yet so that he cannot

find out what God has done from the beginning to the end." Ecclesiastes 3:11 ESV

God put a longing in every human heart to find and fulfill the purpose of life. We are beautifully and wonderfully made. We each have a unique fingerprint, because we are each special to God. The only issue we have is a longing for eternal life, because Adam and Eve's fall in the garden separated us from our Heavenly Father. Every single person has an emptiness that they try to fill through many avenues. We try to fill that void with education, money, power, physical appearance, drugs, alcohol, sex, possessions, etc. However, all the things in this life that the world has to offer will bring us to a dead end at some point.

MY DEAD END CAME BY ADDICTION, DISCOURAGEMENT, UNFULFILLED EXPECTATIONS, DROPPING OUT OF COLLEGE, DROPPING OUT OF TECHNICAL SCHOOL, AND LOSING MY WAY IN LIFE AS I KNEW IT.

I call this the wilderness that leads to eternal life, because it makes us seek out the meaning of life, and it's where I felt my way blindly towards a God I never knew.

Look at Acts 17:26-27

"And he made from one man every nation of mankind to live on all the face of the earth, having determined allotted periods and the boundaries of their dwelling place, 27 that they should seek God, and perhaps feel

their way toward him and find him. Yet he is actually not far from each one of us." Acts 17:26-27 ESV

If this book finds you in this first wilderness, away from God, then I pray what I share with you will help you locate yourself and be drawn to Jesus. He is the only one who can bring you out of this wilderness that leads to eternal death and lead you into eternal life. Like the man said in John 9:25, after Jesus healed him, **"All I know is that I was blind, and now I see!"** I truly have had that kind of experience and I know Jesus wants that for you.

I want to make it clear I have not arrived as a spiritual giant. I do not have all the answers. Some things I will never understand, and I will not stand as a judge on anyone else's faith walk. My assignment with this book is to share my heart and life to encourage you!

I could not have written this book five years ago, or even one year ago. I was not ready. I am also just as sure that in ten years I will add to it; however, now is the time! It has taken over three decades of walking with Jesus to get here.

May you stand on my shoulders and go further than me. May my insight help give you foresight.

I hope this book will be a survival guide through your personal wilderness experiences. I pray the lessons I have learned will bring hope, comfort, understanding, and growth in your life.

- Mike Robinson

Introduction

YOUR PERSONAL SURVIVAL GUIDE

My life is God's story for God's glory. It's really not about what He has done, it's about who He is. He is Love, He is faithful, and He is always near. Psalm 46:1 says, God is a very present help in time of need. It translates into this: when we are in the most need; He is the closest to us. I am not sharing a theory with you in this book. I am sharing personal experiences, personal answers to prayer, and personal struggles in my faith that have caused me to stand through my personal wilderness experiences for over three decades. I pray this will be a survival guide of faith for you as you live out your story for God's glory.

THE ENTRYWAY TO THE WILDERNESS

Chapter 1

THE NECESSARY JOURNEY

The year 2020 found me not only walking around talking to myself, but also shaking my head in disbelief! Just like everyone else, I watched daily events unfold with COVID, injustices in our world, the political unrest, the hypocrisy of a post-Christian nation, and a plethora of inaccurate news. Unlike everyone else, I was experiencing my personal struggles that had started years before.

No one ever told me about the wilderness as a Christian or as a minister. For a long time I felt weird in this season. It seemed taboo to talk about at a pastor's gathering, or even in the church. For me, the wilderness seemed compounded by the condemnation I put on myself for my lack of faith. I rebuked it. I tried to deny it, because I didn't realize that the wilderness is not only normal, it's a necessary journey!

> **THE TRYING OF OUR FAITH IS A RITE OF PASSAGE TO SPIRITUAL GROWTH AND MATURITY.**

We all must walk through the wilderness for at least one season of our lives. We can not become the person God created us to be without it.

A WILDERNESS FROM THE VERY BEGINNING

I grew up in a small town in the Appalachian Mountains of Western Maryland. Some people would call that a wilderness in itself.

Saturday, March 7th, 1964, was the day I was miraculously born. After my older sister was born with mild Rh disease, the doctors advised my parents that they should not have more children. My father had a failed vasectomy from a doctor that assured him failures never happened. Then my mom became pregnant with me. When it came time for her to give birth and I was born, my dad and grandmother said I was tiny and orange looking. From the doctor's perspective, I would not live, and he did not even attempt to prolong my life. Then my father said, "**He is moving!**" The doctor still insisted that I would not live, and they should just wait a few minutes for me to die. That was not good enough for my dad and grandmother, so they took me by car on a bed pillow to another hospital 40 miles away. That hospital gave me the maximum of three blood transfusions.

My dad, who wasn't a praying man, went outside the hospital and asked God for a sign that I would live. After his prayer, a star fell from the sky. He went back and announced to my grandmother, **"He is going to live."**

From there, I led a pretty normal childhood, except for many illnesses and doctors putting me on blood pressure medicine at twelve years old. Despite my illnesses, I was above average at football and played basketball throughout high school. After my 11th grade year, I partied hard, and for the next 7 years I began to really search for meaning, moving around from place to place. I tried things such as community college, technical school, and West Virginia University (thinking of a career in food service management) going the registered dietician/business management route; however, I ended up majoring in partying and being lost in the wilderness. I also searched in relationships, drugs, and religions, but mostly spent my time high, and working as a bouncer/bartender. I had absolutely no identity.

THE BRIGHTER SIDE "ISH"

During the end of this sin-filled season, I met the girl who would later become my wife. On a visit back to my hometown, I saw her picture in a mirror at the local beauty shop and asked, **"who is that girl?"** My next words shocked me. I said, **"I am going to marry her!"** I know that sounds strange, but it happened. When I first met Sandy, she was a backslidden Christian, and after we got married, things were good, but within months, my grandfather died and I went on a drinking binge, and it brought things quickly to a head.

After that, she told me she was committing her life fully to Christ again, and He was going to be first. I could join her or leave and I knew I was at a major crossroads. At that time, I was a truck driver on the road and all I could think about as I would drive was my emptiness and how much I had messed up life. From that time I started continually drinking and using drugs to cope with the constant battle of depression.

THE TURN AROUND

One day, I got home right before Sandy went to a revival service at her grandfather's church. I was in a major tug of war with good and evil and yet in spite of that war, I went with her. That night I had a radical encounter with Jesus Christ and I surrendered my whole life to Him and made a commitment to be His and at His disposal for anything He wanted me to do. I promised I would serve Him with the same zeal I used to party with! With this commitment to Him, I felt an enormous relief from everything I had carried for so long. All my sins were forgiven, and I felt new and alive!

I FELT ACCEPTED AND NORMAL IN THE PRESENCE OF JESUS.

For the first time in my life, I felt like I fit in by just being me! I was home! I was a new creation in Christ (2 Corinthians 5:17). Jesus changed my life forever. I was fabulously saved!

God then brought a 19-year-old pastor and his wife, Keith and Darla Collins, and their two little girls, Amber and Ashton, into our lives. We have become lifelong friends (more like family) for decades now. Looking back, we were all just kids, but we were on fire for God. They may have looked at it differently, but they were a godsend to our small town of Friendsville, MD.

THE CALL

After about 10 months, Keith and Darla left Friendsville, and the church asked me to fill the pulpit. I would have said no, but two things happened from God I could not deny. First, God had given me dreams of preaching behind that pulpit at that little church. Second, a pastor friend of Keith's from Ohio had given me a prophecy 30 days prior, saying, **"Within 30 days, souls will be saved through your hands."**

It's also amazing to note that when I received that word of prophecy at church, I was in the middle of purchasing a gas station and garage business. The loan was approved, and I already had signs made for the business. However, the night before I signed the papers, a man called and warned us not to make the purchase because of a problem. So we cancelled the deal. That next Sunday, I was asked to step in and pastor the church.

One year after being saved, a 26-year-old who could never make a speech in school, an ex-heathen and bouncer in a bar, became a pastor. It's crazy, but it's true! I was ordained on September 2, 1990, and it's been a wild ride ever since for the glory of God!

THE PREPARATION

In the first weeks, I prayed about going to Bible college, however; I sensed the Lord prompting me to spend 40 hours a week with Him for 2 years. My own Bible plan was to read 7 chapters each day from one book of the Bible, or that entire book of the Bible. In those 2 years, I read the Bible 4 1/3 times, and studied five thousand one hundred and ten chapters. No one had taught me to study the Bible, so I started with a highlighter, a King James Bible, a Strong's Concordance, and a Webster's Dictionary (there was no Google or internet). I started at Genesis and ended in Revelation. I highlighted every word I did not understand and studied it. Needless to say, I highlighted almost every word in my first Bible.

When it came to prayer, I took Matthew 6:6 quite literally, it says,

> *"But you, when you pray, go into your room, and when you have shut your door, pray to your Father who is in the secret place; and your Father who sees in secret will reward you openly." Matthew 6:6 NKJV*

So I built a prayer closet in the basement, painted a cross on the wall, and stood against that cross many times. I didn't understand the wilderness experiences, so I would stand with my arms outstretched against the cross and cry out to Jesus. After a short time, my arms would shake. Ultimately, I would drop them.

Many times I would end up on my knees, realizing I could never have been crucified like Jesus. I would just worship Him. Through that, He gave me the strength to go on, but I still did not understand the wilderness. It looked like every other Christian was doing better than me. I felt flawed. I quit many times in my head. I just never told anyone.

It seemed to me like everyone was passing me. Every other church and pastor seemed to move, and I seemed stuck in the wilderness. I asked the Lord why I was going so slow and I sensed Him say, **"You can have it quick or right?"** I chose right, because I knew right was right. However, even though I knew it was the right choice, it still felt bad to my flesh.

Little did I know at the time that following Christ and wanting my life and character to be right would mean walking through the wilderness.

EVERY CHRISTIAN MUST WALK THROUGH THE WILDERNESS.

'Then Jesus was led up by the Spirit into the wilderness to be tempted by the devil.' Matthew 4:1 NKJV

One thing that was a big help during this time was finding out the Holy Spirit had led Jesus into the wilderness for 40 days and nights to be tempted. I know days can be very difficult; however nights were the worst for me and seeing that Jesus overcame being tempted **day and night,** gave me hope.

"For I know the thoughts that I think toward you, says the Lord, thoughts of peace and not of evil, to give you a future and a hope." Jeremiah 29:11 NKJV

I pray that gives you hope as well because even though the wilderness is necessary, it is not the final destination that God has for you. There is hope and there is a future.

Chapter 2

DAVID'S SECRET WILDERNESS WEAPON

In over 3 decades of pastoring in the small wilderness town I grew up in, there is a passage I have preached on many times. At about year 26 of ministry I really began to question God about this passage, because it bothered me so much. It was one that challenged me, but I could never get a working application of it in my life.

> *And David was greatly distressed; for the people spake of stoning him, because the soul of all the people was grieved, every man for his sons and for his daughters: but David encouraged himself in the Lord his God. 1 Samuel 30:6 KJV*

Way before this tragedy happened in the life of David, he was anointed by the prophet Samuel to be the next king of Israel, but instead of going straight to the throne room, he ended up in a wilderness place of desperation. I could relate to that; however, unlike me, he overcame and had victory.

This will make you scratch your head even more, the tragedy we read about in vs. 6 wasn't just because people were opposing him, but it was partially his own fault. David was not in the place he should have been and he was out fighting a battle that he shouldn't have been fighting. While he was out, his house was burned, his family was taken, and his loyal men were now thinking of stoning him. In spite of all of this he still experienced victory in the end. That just does not seem fair, why is he still experiencing victory even in the middle of his self inflicted tragedy?

After years of study and prayer, I finally realized that David learned something in the field as a shepherd boy that helped him win battles throughout his entire life, because he faced the lion, the bear, the giant, Saul's attempts to destroy him and those closest to him, and now his family being taken hostage and his tribe blamed him and wanted to kill him.

This sounds like a small town pastor's life (tongue in cheek); however, there was a big difference between David and I. What did David do that I was not doing? Did he throw up his hands and quit? **NO, David encouraged himself in the Lord!**

DAVID WAS ENCOURAGED AND I WAS DISCOURAGED.

I cried out to Jesus in my desperation and said, **"I want to start over like I have never been a Christian or a Pastor, and like I never knew You!"**

I SENSED THE LORD SAYING, "THAT'S GOOD, BECAUSE A KNOW IT ALL CAN'T GROW AT ALL!"

I cried out to Jesus, **"Show me what David learned in the wilderness and what YOU had in the wilderness that got YOU through!"**

LEARNING TO WALK BY FAITH

At that moment, and for the next 3 weeks, I would not only get the outline of this book, but so much more. I would get a manuscript for victory in the wilderness. I believe this has not only helped me, but it will help everyone who reads it.

David learned how to encourage himself in the Lord by learning to really walk in the principles of faith. Like David, we must learn to build our own faith. I heard someone say once, **"A stone didn't actually kill Goliath. David's faith did!"** It's true! We walk, talk, live, and defeat giants in the wilderness through faith.

NO QUICK FIX

I have found through the wilderness that there are no quick fixes. We can't scroll down through our wilderness like social media and find all the answers. The wilderness is about a deep work, gaining maturity, and growing up. It combines the trying of our faith, the purification of every motive and attitude, and a renewing of the mind until we are so established in the love of God we reflect Jesus no matter if we are in a wilderness or not.

When we practice the principles of faith over and over again, it turns into the Spirit of faith. It is just like the Bible says in 2 Corinthians 4:13

> *"And since we have the same spirit of faith, according to what is written, "I believed and therefore I spoke," we also believe and therefore speak." 2 Corinthians 4:13 NKJV*

When we build our faith, though God's Word, and practice the principles, our faith grows like a muscle. We read the Word with prayer; we speak the Word in faith; we listen to the Word with a hungry heart; we renew our mind to the Word (Romans 12:1-2); we fight unbelief with the Word, and we maintain a heart of thankfulness and praise! Soon our heart, our head, and our mouth will line up.

Please hear me Christians. We have to stand in this hour like no other. **We must without arrogance, mature to the place we are confident of who we are in Christ!**

QUESTIONS TO CONSIDER:

1. Have you been through the wilderness that leads you to God? If so, what was your dead end in the wilderness?

2. Are you presently in a wilderness season? If so, press into the pages of this book and ask God to speak to you through it.

Chapter 3

BE LIKE A TREE

"The strongest oak tree in the forest was once a little nut who held its ground!"............ Unknown

The day I cried out to Jesus, **"Show me what David learned in the wilderness and what YOU had in the wilderness that got You through!"**

I sensed the Lord saying, **"BE LIKE A TREE!"**

Ok, **"Be like a tree?"** My thoughts immediately went to the huge oak on our ministry property. Before ever thinking about buying the property, someone had prayed over me and said my life and ministry would be like that of a mighty oak. When we saw the oak tree on the grounds where our church is now, it was a confirmation that we were in the right place. The oak would go through many storms, and even though it would bend and carry many scars, it would not break. I have even witnessed our 108 foot tall oak take minimal damage as other trees were destroyed by a tornado coming through our town.

I AM THAT TREE THAT BRINGS HIM JOY

It has been true, as my wife, Sandy, and I look back over our life, we have had to stand through storms, both physically and mentally; through storms of betrayal, grief, misunderstanding, storms in our finances, and on and on and on, but by God's grace we are still standing. In fact, through these storms, we learned to depend on His grace even more.

One day I was at the church praying and looking out the cafe window at the oak tree. I said, **"Lord, I really have done nothing great for You in my life."** I sensed the Lord saying, **"See that oak tree? It has no beautiful flowers or delicious fruit. It simply brings Me joy by standing! That's what you**

do for Me." In fact, that's what every Christian does when they just stand for Jesus. Just like the acorn being planted is a little thing, but it becomes a big tree.

WHEN WE PLANT OURSELVES WHERE GOD WANTS US AND STAND STRONG REGARDLESS OF ANY STORMS WE FACE, IT BRINGS HIM GREAT GLORY, AND THAT'S ALL THAT REALLY MATTERS.

I am writing this for everyone God created to stand and be the tree God created you to be.

HALLMARK

Last year, I received a Hallmark card from Billy and Linda (one of the most precious couples in our church). They said, "If there was ever a card written just for you, this is it."

THE OAK TREE
A message of Encouragement
A mighty wind blew night and day.
It stole the oak tree's leaves away,
Then it snapped its boughs and pulled its bark
Until the Oak was tired and stark.
But still the Oak tree held its ground
While other trees fell all around.

The weary wind gave up and spoke,
"How can you still be standing, Oak?"
The oak tree said, "I know that you

Can break each branch of mine in two,
Carry every leaf away,
Shake my limbs and make me sway.

But I have roots stretched in the earth,
Growing stronger since my birth.
You'll never touch them, for you see,
They are the deepest part of me.

Until today, I wasn't sure
Of just how much I could endure.
But now I've found, with thanks to you,
I am stronger than I ever knew.

This card really touched me, because it just fell in line with everything the Master has been speaking to me about life. It is a powerful reminder that no matter what comes against us on the outside, if our roots are secure in Jesus Christ, we will make it through any storm!

After thinking of the Oak Tree on our property, two key scriptures come to mind. Psalm 1:1-3 and Isaiah 61:1-3.

Blessed is the man who walks not in the counsel of the
ungodly, nor stands in the path of sinners, nor sits in the
seat of the scornful; 2 But his delight is in the law of the
Lord, and in His law, he meditates day and night. 3 He
shall be like a tree planted by the rivers of water that
bring forth its fruit in its season, whose leaf also shall not

wither; and whatever he does shall prosper. Psalm 1:1-3 NKJV

LISTEN TO THE RIGHT VOICES

The direction for the wilderness is so clear from God; however, when you can't see the forest for the trees, it gets blurry. Psalm 1:1 clearly says, don't listen to or follow ungodly counsel. The way to blessing in the wilderness is to listen to the right voice and walk in the right way. This lines up exactly with what Jesus did in His wilderness experience (Matthew 4:1-11). Satan brought Him ungodly counsel, but Jesus didn't follow it. Jesus followed God's Word, no matter what. Ungodly counsel will cause you to walk in the wrong way and walk after the wrong things and you will get lost in the wilderness. When fear speaks to you, it's ungodly counsel. When you listen to fear and get intimidated, you have walked in the counsel of the ungodly. When faith speaks to you, or through you, it is godly counsel! Walking in Faith is walking in the counsel of the Godly!

FOLLOW THE RIGHT PEOPLE

Then God says, "Don't stand in the path of sinners". It is a rut in the road that will lead to sin and death. We are supposed to cross that path to reach sinners, but not stay there. Dietreict BonHoeffer said, "**May we be enabled to say "NO" to sin and "YES" to the sinner.**"

SPEAK THE RIGHT WORDS

After that, God tells us not to sit in the seat of the scornful because that will cause you to be critical, judgmental, and a mocker of the things of God. We must guard against this. Judah Glenn, one of our first mentors who had been a missionary for 56 years, said, "**Mike, you will build nothing for God by pulling a stone out of another man's foundation.**"

This is good insight on knowing the will of God! Notice God tells us where not to walk, stand or sit. If you want to know where not to sleep,, and who not to sleep with, the Bible has a lot of good info on that too! (just in case you don't already know, haha).

"But his delight is in the law of the Lord, and in His law, he meditates day and night. He shall be like a tree planted by the rivers of water that bring forth its fruit in its season, whose leaf also shall not wither; and whatever he does shall prosper." Psalm 1:2-3 NKJV

I AM LIKE A TREE

"Be like a tree." Say it with me, **"I shall be like a tree, planted by the rivers of water, fruitful in my season, ever green, and never empty."**

The second scripture I thought of was Isaiah 61:1-3 which states,

The Spirit of the Sovereign Lord is on me because the Lord has anointed me to proclaim good news to the poor. He has sent me to bind up the brokenhearted, to proclaim freedom for the captives and release from darkness for the prisoners, to proclaim the year of the Lord's favor and the day of vengeance of our God, to comfort all who mourn, and provide for those who grieve in Zion – to give on them a crown of beauty instead of ashes, the oil of joy instead of mourning, and a garment of praise instead of a spirit of despair. **They will be called oaks of righteousness, a planting of the Lord for the display of his splendor**. *Isaiah 61:1-3 NIV emphasis added.*

One of my favorite quotes is,

"THE STRONGEST OAK TREE IN THE FOREST WAS ONCE A LITTLE NUT WHO HELD ITS GROUND!"............ UNKOWN

To think that the massive mighty oak tree at our ministry center, that is believed to be over 260 years old and was recently named Grand Champion White Oak in Garrett County, and 13th in the state of Maryland, came from a tiny acorn!

White Oaks are one of the most prestigious trees in the USA. All of their strength started in a tiny acorn the size of an unborn baby at 6-8 weeks old. Just like us, we are so tiny when we are born, but God has planned for us to be planted, and grow strong and tall through the seasons of life.

IT'S JUST THAT SIMPLE

I have to believe my life and calling are just this simple: I'm just the little nut from Friendsville, Maryland, who held my ground! And I also believe your life and call is just that simple! I encourage you to dig in and hold your ground even if everyone around you thinks you are a nut. Remember, there is a mighty oak inside of you that only God has seen the end of.

Remember this: You can ignore a nut, tramp on it, and grind it in the ground, but when it takes root and grows into an oak tree, you can't ignore it any longer. It's a force to be reckoned with.

AN OAK IS STRONG AND RESILIENT IN THE TOUGHEST STORMS.

I can tell you from personal experience why oak trees are considered "hard wood". When I was in my early 20s, I was cutting down an oak tree with a chain saw. The wind caught the tree and blew it into another oak, causing a limb to break and fall 70 feet on to my head. An oak limb is harder than a human head. After a visit to the E.R., a concussion, and stitches, I conceded I fought the tree and the tree won!

GROWTH HAPPENS OVER TIME

Just like a tree has rings to measure a year's growth we also measure our growth over time. Every year tells a story, and while not every year may look great, we can not let a season we go through define us, because God is the Author and finisher of your story and He makes all things work for our good (Romans 8:28). He knows the end from the beginning, and a "bad season" in life is not the end of our life. My wife Sandy tells me, **"Mike, your life is God's story for His glory!"**

BE LIKE A TREE

These pictures below of God's creation are mind blowing when you consider God said we would BE LIKE A TREE! This makes me in awe of God!

It is amazing how God, being the Creator of everything, illustrates the importance of this scripture in Isaiah all throughout nature! He must really want us to understand just who we are, and how much strength we have when we are connected to

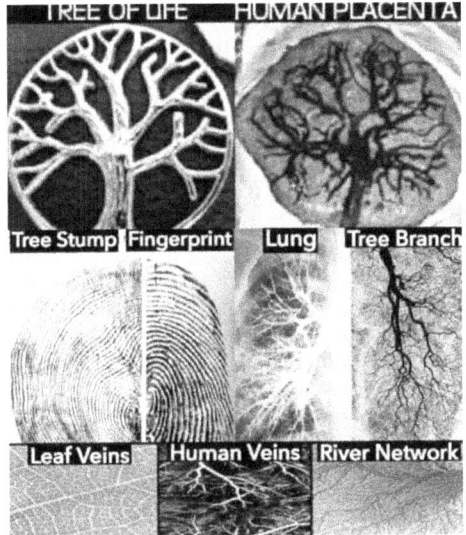

Him! He shows us in the rings of a tree, the tree branch, the veins in a leaf, the uniqueness of the fingerprint, the human

veins, the human placenta, the lung, an aerial view of the river network, and the tree of life. Psalm 66:4 says,

> *"Everything on earth will worship you: they will sing your praises, shouting your name in glorious songs." Psalm 66:4 NLT*

I can just see the trees bowing down in the wind to worship God, and the song it must make as all creation worships Him. When I look at all God created, it causes me to Worship Him and sing praises with my voice! It blows me away how God orchestrated everything in the universe to reveal HIMSELF and His love for us! All we have to do is look around for it in what He has created! As Hebrews 4:12 states, His Word is alive all around us.

This same God gave us each a unique fingerprint, and He has a specific plan for each of us.

Bill Johnson said, "**God is responsible for having a plan for your life, but you are responsible for your participation in His plan.**"

We can be unengaged with God, unthankful, disobedient, and proud and have slow growth, or be intimate, thankful, obedient, and humble and have strong growth! Either way, the wilderness is part of every journey.

Larry Randoff said, "**God will fulfill all His promises, but He is not obligated to fulfill your potential!**"

I have said many times,

"YOU CAN'T HAVE MICROWAVE MATURITY AND EXPECT CONCRETE CHARACTER!" IT TAKES A PROCESS.

I promise you that God has a great call on your life, but you will never reach your full potential without going through a process. Just like a cake takes heat to bake, and gold takes fire to be purified, for you to be a mighty tree that will stand, it takes a process over time to mature. There are no short cuts.

QUESTIONS TO CONSIDER:

1. Are you ready to commit yourself to being like a tree no matter what type of tree it is, if God gets the glory?

2. Is there any ungodly counsel in your life that doesn't line up with God's Word which you need to stop following?

3. Are you in a rut, and standing on a path of sinners, or are you on the narrow way of the Lord that leads through the wilderness to victory? (Matthew 7:13-14)

4. Have you sat in the seat of the scornful today and been frustrated, critical, and judgmental? If so, this is a time before you go any further to repent and return to your First Love. It's time to look at all these

questions seriously and decide to be committed to being like a tree that will stand.

* I suggest you pray here and now. Write the time and date below and then proceed to the next chapter.

Section 2

GROWTH AND MATURITY IN THE WILDERNESS

In the next 6 chapters, we will explore six things that affect the growth and maturity of a tree and how it pertains to our lives. Soil, Drought, Storms, Pest and Insects, Forest Fire, and Sickness and Disease.

Chapter 4

SOIL

Soil: the upper layer of earth where plants grow. For our illustration soil will represent the heart of a person.

> *"Ultimately, the way we finish is what matters, but where a seed starts has a lot to do with how a tree ends up. The soil has to be right for the tree to be its best." Mike Robinson*

In the sower's parable (Matthew 13:1-23), Jesus taught us that the growth of a seed is influenced by where it is planted. Some seeds fall along the path, some fall on rocky ground, some among thorns, and still other seeds fall on good soil. Birds devour the seed on the path and consequently never gets covered by the soil because it never gets planted. The seed on the rocky ground comes up quickly because the soil is shallow, but when the sun comes out, the seedlings are scorched and wither away because they have no root. Other seeds fall among thorns, which choke out the seedlings. Lastly. some seed finds good soil and become life's finishers.

This parable is relevant to every life because everyone has the potential to produce all God has planned for them. However, many miss everything God has for them because their hearts are not good ground.

THE GOOD NEWS IS, THE GROUND OF YOUR HEART DOESN'T HAVE TO STAY IN ITS CURRENT CONDITION. NO ONE IS BEYOND GOD'S REACH!

The reason the seed on the path becomes bird food is because people hear the message of God's Kingdom, but do not understand it. Because they don't understand what they are hearing, the evil one snatches the seed that was sown in their heart.

The reason the seed on the rocky ground fails is because it has no depth, and the roots are scorched by the sun. They receive the Word with joy, but when trouble or persecution come because of the Word, they quickly fall away!

The seed sown among thorns is the one who hears the Word, but the worries of this life and the deceitfulness of wealth choke the Word and it becomes unfruitful.

The seed on good soil hears and understands the Word. They bear fruit. They are not sampling or just trying out God's Word to see if it works; they believe it and act on it.

Every promise of God is what we would call a seed. When we read or hear about what God says in His Word, what happens next has a lot to do with the condition the soil of our heart is in.

Three essential nutrients needed for good soil of our heart are humility, thankfulness, and faith!

KEEPING YOUR SOIL RIGHT

When I ponder my life in the secret place before God, I don't see a ministry title or accomplishments. If I could compare myself to any great people in the Bible, it wouldn't be a great Apostle or Prophet, it would be the woman with the alabaster box. I believe the posture of her heart is one that we should never stray from.

In Luke 7:36-50, we read her story.

> *"Then one of the Pharisees invited Jesus to eat with him, and He entered the Pharisee's house and reclined at the table. When a sinful woman from that town learned that Jesus was dining there, she brought an alabaster jar of perfume. As she stood behind Him at His feet weeping, she began to wet His feet with her tears and wipe them with her hair. Then she kissed His feet and anointed them with the perfume. When the Pharisee who had invited*

Jesus saw this, he said to himself, "If this man were a prophet, He would know who this is and what kind of woman is touching Him—for she is a sinner!" But Jesus answered him, "Simon, I have something to tell you." "Tell me, Teacher," he said. "Two men were debtors to a certain moneylender. One owed him five hundred denarii, and the other fifty. When they were unable to repay him, he forgave both of them. Which one, then, will love him more?" "I suppose the one who was forgiven more," Simon replied. "You have judged correctly," Jesus said. And turning toward the woman, He said to Simon, "Do you see this woman? When I entered your house, you did not give me water for my feet, but she wet my feet with her tears and wiped them with her hair. You did not greet me with a kiss, but she has not stopped kissing my feet since I arrived. You did not anoint my head with oil, but she has anointed My feet with perfume. Therefore I tell you, because her many sins have been forgiven, she has loved much. But he who has been forgiven little loves little." Then, Jesus said to her, "Your sins are forgiven." But those at the table began to say to themselves, "Who is this who even forgives sins?" And Jesus told the woman, "Your faith has saved you; go in peace." Luke 7:36-50 NKJV

She is humble. She is thankful. She is faithful and full of faith. It's important that I always go back to her when I struggle. It keeps my soil right; it keeps my heart right. It will keep your heart right as well. As a Christian, I never want to lose sight of the fact that it's a privilege and honor to pour out our lives for Jesus. He has loved us, saved us, forgiven us and forever makes intercession for us. He stands with us. He is faithful, even when we are not faithful to Him. He is faithful to us.

"If we are faithless, He remains faithful; He cannot deny Himself." 2 Timothy 2:13 NKJV

HUMILITY

Look at her humility! She shows up as an outcast in this crowd. In Luke 7:38, she stood behind Jesus weeping; she bows at His feet and wets His feet with her tears (tears of thankfulness) and wipes His feet with her hair. Then she kisses His feet and anoints them with perfume that has cost her everything. This is always mind blowing to me.

I was just like her. I stood behind Jesus, weeping. My pain and sin were overwhelming. His love drew me to bow at His feet when I found out His forgiveness was for me. Then in 1989, I knelt and cried and cried and cried at His feet and proclaimed, "**Whatever I can do for you, Lord, I surely will!**" It was the first time I felt completely normal. With Jesus, I discovered an everlasting place I never wish to depart.

Today when you read this, I pray that if you're behind

Jesus weeping, you would find your place of forgiveness and freedom before Him as I did.

I also pray if anything has come between you and that place you belong at His feet, you would settle that now and return to your first love and joy.

> **HUMILITY MAKES RICH SOIL CONDUCIVE TO AN ABUNDANT HARVEST.**

I have said many times, "**You can't just add Jesus to your life like you add cream to your coffee. It just doesn't work like that.**" We must be all in.

> *"Therefore, lay aside all filthiness and overflow of wickedness, and receive with meekness the implanted word, which is able to save your souls." James 1:21 NKJV*

We must receive the seed of God's Word with a meek and humble heart. For lasting growth and fruit, we have to humble ourselves. We can't act like we know everything.

> **REMEMBER, SOMEONE WHO KNOWS IT ALL CAN'T GROW AT ALL!**

The Bible says,

> *"Therefore, humble yourselves under the mighty hand of God, that He may exalt you in due time." 1 Peter 5:6 NKJV*

THANKFULNESS

The first nutrient in the soil is humility, the second is thankfulness. I have learned that thankfulness is a reason I have overcome every test in my life, named in the Parable of The Sower. From the birds taking me out when I knew nothing yet, to the sun scorching my roots, to the persecution from people, to worries for this life, and deceitfulness of riches taking me out: a thankful heart has grounded me.

THE WAY WE BECOME A CHRIST FOLLOWER IN THE FIRST PLACE HAS EVERYTHING TO DO WITH COMPLETING LIFE AS A CHRIST FOLLOWER.

I started following Him because I realized I was a sinner and I needed a savior. I could not save myself. I had tried everything I knew, and I was empty and I actually felt lost. The party life didn't do it. The fast cars didn't do it. The relationships I had didn't do it. Sports and hobbies didn't do it. I looked at Buddhism, Mormonism, and I even tried the church. The problem was I never tried Jesus Himself and I didn't know who He really is. Psalm 34:8 says, "**Taste the Lord and see that he is Good...**"

I thought believing Jesus existed was the same thing as believing in Jesus. I was wrong. A man told me one day that demons believe Jesus exists and they tremble at His Word, but they are not saved. They can't be saved and they can't go to heaven. (James 2:19-20). He said, you can't go to heaven either by just believing Jesus exists. You must know Him (John 17:3).

Wow! That hit me hard. When my wife took me to church, I thought she sat me in the front on purpose and told the preacher what to say to me. He told me that every person is born a sinner, and no matter how good or bad we are, one sin makes us a sinner. He then said that sin separates us from God. That sin nailed Jesus to the cross. My sin. While I was still a sinner, Jesus was dying for me because He loved me so much. He would forgive me for every sin and give me a new start.

> **I FINALLY GOT IT! THE SOIL OF MY HEART HAD BEEN PREPARED. I REALIZED THAT NIGHT MY SIN NAILED HIM TO THE CROSS.**

I went forward and knelt at a wooden altar and cried and cried and cried as waves of forgiveness washed away my sins. I felt the weight of the world lift from my shoulder for the first time. I gave Jesus more than my heart. I gave Him my life. I've always said I got a better deal than Jesus, because I came with nothing but sin and my broken life. He gave me everything! He gave me a new life. I am eternally thankful. I recently said, "**If I were a cat, I would give Jesus all 9 lives because it's the best thing I ever did.**"

Look again what Jesus said in Luke 7:47,

"Therefore I say to you, her sins, which are many, are forgiven, for she loved much. But to whom little is forgiven, the same loves little." Luke 7:47 NKJV

When you realize how much you were forgiven, that much thankfulness will keep you for eternity.

FAITH

The last ingredient is faith, because without faith it's impossible to please God (Hebrews 11:6), without faith it's impossible to have good soil.

"For indeed the gospel was preached to us as well as to them; but the word which they heard did not profit them, not being mixed with faith in those who heard it." Hebrews 4:2 NKJV

Faith has to be mixed in our soil. I will get into the subject of faith in further detail later.

THE RED TOWEL

As humans in a fallen world, it can be so easy to lose these three elements of humility, thankfulness, and faith that make the soil of our heart good ground and exchange them for pride, ungratefulness, and fear. That is why we must keep our eyes fixed on Jesus.

If you ever see me carrying a red towel, there is a reason. One day I was very stressed about meeting with someone about ministry issues. For years I worried too much. I was overly concerned I would cause a relationship to be broken or hurt if I confronted them. I know it was my personal identity issue. The Lord dealt with me about my motives. He showed me that my motive was pure, because I hoped to teach them to obey God, not just obey me. It freed me. I went and bought a red towel (red to represent the blood of Jesus), and I used it that next day at the meeting. In the meeting, I sensed the Lord wanting me to place the towel on their feet, so my wife and I knelt down and prayed over them. I am not sure what it did for them, but something broke in us. From that day until now, when I pray or preach or go to a meeting, I remember that my only motive when I speak is to wash the feet of Jesus and wash the feet of the people I speak to. Carrying this towel reminds me to be humble, thankful and faithful to speak what I know I need to. Like the woman with the alabaster box, I become more concerned about worshipping Jesus than self, or what people think. It frees me to truly serve!

When God's seed is planted in a humble, thankful, faithful heart, it will yield 100 fold!

QUESTIONS TO CONSIDER:

1. Have you given Jesus your heart or your whole life?

2. Which soil types have you experienced in your walk with God? The path, the rocky, the thorny or the

good soil? Explain with personal examples, this will help you stay steady in the future.

3. In what ways are you eternally thankful?

4. In what ways could you be more thankful?

5. What is your story of God's forgiveness that you could share with others?

Chapter 5

DROUGHT

Drought: "a period of dryness, especially when prolonged specifically; one that causes extensive damage to crops or prevents their successful growth." Drought for our illustration will represent dry times in our lives, times of wilderness, and/or times of temptation.

> *"While trees can generally respond to variable rainfall, drought creates a stress that exacerbates other problems. Specifically, trees that were already stressed by some other issue, like poor soils or insect infestation, are likely to decline even more following a drought. Trees that went into the drought in good shape will be stressed and may become more susceptible to disease problems or other pests." From the North Dakota State University*

article (Drought and Trees: What to expect and what to do. 2020)

In Luke 4:1-15, we see Jesus being led into the wilderness by The Holy Spirit. Let's read it before I point out a few things Jesus did that will work for all of us.

"And Jesus, full of the Holy Spirit, returned from the Jordan and was led by the Spirit in the wilderness for forty days, being tempted by the devil. And he ate nothing during those days. And when they were ended, he was hungry. The devil said to him, "If you are the Son of God, command this stone to become bread." And Jesus answered him, "It is written, 'Man shall not live by bread alone.'" And the devil took him up and showed him all the kingdoms of the world in a moment of time, and said to him, "To you I will give all this authority and their glory, for it has been delivered to me, and I give it to whom I will. If you, then, will worship me, it will all be yours." And Jesus answered him, "It is written, "'You shall worship the Lord your God, and him only shall you serve.'" And he took him to Jerusalem and set him on the pinnacle of the temple and said to him, "If you are the Son of God, throw yourself down from here, for it is written, "'He will command his angels concerning you, to guard you,' and "'On their hands they will bear you up, lest you strike your foot against a stone.'" And Jesus answered him, "It is said, 'You shall not put the Lord your God to the test.'" And when the devil had ended every

temptation, he departed from him until an opportune time." Luke 4:1-13 ESV

Here is a verse by verse synopsis.

VERSE 2

In verse two, we see Jesus fasted forty days and nights. He was tempted the whole time by the enemy, and we can leave it up to our imagination that the things we are tempted with came at Jesus also. Just thinking about that blesses me, because when I feel alone in my wilderness temptations, I can know from this verse that Jesus has been where we are or will be. He has been tempted like us, yet without sin.

Then it says, "He was hungry." I can relate to that. I am always hungry. I don't have to be fasting. My first ten day fast on water, I was very naïve. My friend Keith was fasting, so I asked him if I could do it, too. I had never even heard of it before. Keith gave me some very simple instructions. I went on this fast, knowing three things: First, eat nothing. Second, at mealtime, read the Bible and pray. Third, don't let people know you are fasting. Keith also added a bonus. He said we could have a LifeSaver mint or Tic-tac mint at church services so we didn't have bad breath. It's funny now, but we were after God, full of zeal and child-like faith.

I had been working a sales job in an office, but on the

day we started to fast, my boss decided we would go to his property and clear trees. The first two days were hard, but I made it. We didn't have bottled water like today, so I drank very little. Only at lunchtime and after work. On the third day, I was running a chain saw, and I had a vision. It wasn't the God kind of vision. I saw fumes coming up from the ground, and I passed out under a tree. My boss came running and said, **"What's wrong?"** I said, **"I passed out from not eating."** He said, **"Why didn't you tell me?"** I said, **"I'm not supposed to tell anyone."** He said, **"Well, what can I do?"**

I yelled, **" Milk Shake! Get me a Chocolate Malt milk shake!"** He took me to get one, and I felt defeated. However, I just started again, and God blessed me even in my ignorance. Looking back at this story is so humorous, but it's true! I told this story, because I want to be transparent about my walk. Truly, every time I fast, I admire Jesus more for His forty-day fast.

VERSES 3 AND 4

When we look back at verse three and four, Satan tempted Jesus to turn a stone into bread. Satan is the epitome of pride, so he thinks he can appeal to pride in Jesus. Satan says, "**IF You are the Son of God?**" Satan always tries to see if we are dead to self or not. He is always going to come at us with the "**IF you are a son or daughter of**

God, then prove it!" He tries to catch us in the flesh. Pride is Satan's hook. When you make a stand, or when you make a declaration to follow God anywhere, Satan will come with an "**IF**" and a "**Prove It**". I have honestly won some and lost some. You already know I would have turned the stone into a milkshake. Look what Jesus did. It's a key to victory in drought. He said, "**IT IS WRITTEN!**" We will see this is major! I get excited when I preach this, and for some reason my voice always booms these three words. "**IT IS WRITTEN**" is the Word of God. The Word of God means victory for us and defeat for Satan. Ephesians 5:26 talks about washing with the water of the Word. I see this as a drink for Jesus and a drowning for the devil. Every time we stand on the Word, we get a drink and the devil gets to drown.

When Jesus says, "**It is written,**" He shows what He feeds on. It's the Word. It is important to note that Jesus didn't just quote the Word, He had the attitude of the Word. Jesus illustrated to us what the spirit of faith looks like in the dessert. He believed and He spoke just like 2 Corinthians 4:13 says.

> *And since we have the same spirit of faith, according to what is written, "I believed and therefore I spoke," we also believe and therefore speak, 2 Corinthians 4:13 NKJV*

VERSES 5 THROUGH 8

In verses five through eight, Satan is at it again. He offers

Jesus power, kingdoms of this world, authority and their glory in exchange for bowing His knee to him in worship. Satan doesn't realize that Jesus knew His identity. Satan offers Jesus a management position when Jesus knows He is the King of all Kings. Jesus didn't need the glory or power of a management position, because all honor and all power and all glory belong to Him. Again, Jesus says out loud, "**IT IS WRITTEN**".

VERSES 9 THROUGH 13

Satan backs up for a minute and then does something that really interests me. It says, "**He took Jesus**." Theologians have differing views on this. Some believe Satan could take Jesus in His mind, through a supernatural power, into an immediate illusion of some sort. Others believe he physically took Jesus by grabbing Him, and translating Him to Jerusalem, and setting Him on the pinnacle of the temple. I can see merit in both. One thing we know is VR (Virtual Reality) and Google did not exist. This isn't salvational, it just interests me.

One night I was ministering to someone who was suicidal, and the Lord had me show them verse nine where Satan said, "**Throw yourself down from here**". I believe Satan was coming at Jesus with a spirit of suicide. He tempted Him to take His life prematurely, and outside of God's plan. When I shared this that night, the man knew for a fact that anything he was thinking, even about suicide, Jesus was in all ways tempted like him. That man broke, and he never committed suicide. Praise God! God hates suicide, and so do I. I have been in such dark places in the wilderness where it would be easier to die than go on, but by God's grace, I tapped into the water of God's Word. You can, too. Never give up.

I currently pray that if you are in that place, you will find encouragement to seek help and be motivated to persevere.

THREE MASTER KEYS

There are three master keys Jesus used in the Wilderness that still work for us today. They are fasting, prayer and the Word of God. Many miss the fasting part when they teach this, but believe me, in our walk in the wilderness, fasting is a key element of our victory.

In every wilderness temptation, there is a way of escape, and there is "water" at your disposal.

The Bible says in John 7:38, "out of our belly would flow rivers of living water". It's a miracle that takes place in everyone born again. It's why the Bible says we are like trees planted by the rivers of water. We will bring forth fruit in our season, despite the drought! Our leaf will not wither and whatever we do will prosper! Remember:

"If there is a wilderness that the Holy Spirit leads you

into, then there is a deeper intimacy God has for you!"
- Mike Robinson

QUESTIONS TO CONSIDER IN DROUGHT:

1. What is the key to victory in drought? (It is written)

2. What is Satan's hook? (Pride)

3. What 2 things do 2 Corinthians 4:13 say we need to do to have the Spirit of faith? (Believe and Speak)

4. Which temptations do you struggle with the most? Look up scriptures on this topic or topics and find a new truth for yourself. John 8:32 says, "you shall know the truth and the truth shall make you free"!

5. Say this Scripture out loud and make it personal.

   "No temptation has overtaken you that is not common to man. God is faithful, and he will not let you be tempted beyond your ability, but with the temptation he will also provide the way of escape, that you may be able to endure it." 1 Corinthians 10:13 ESV

   Now say, "It is written, No temptation has overtaken ME that is not common to man. God is faithful, and He will not let ME be tempted beyond my ability, but with the temptation He will also provide the way of escape, that I may be able to endure it."

Chapter 6

STORMS

STORM: "a violent disturbance of the atmosphere with strong winds and usually rain, thunder, lightning, or snow."

A tree in the wilderness gets no weather reports and does not move to take cover. It has to have a good foundation to withstand the storms of life, and so does every Christian. The foundation or root system is never seen or appreciated until the storm arrives and they are put to the test. The tree can't wait until the storm to get rooted, it must be planted long before it ever arrives.

THE BRIGHT SIDE OF THE STORM

When God tells us to be like a tree, we need to remember that life is not all sunny days and gentle summer rain.

HOWEVER, WITHOUT THE STORMS WE FACE, WE COULD NEVER DEVELOP OR PROVE OUR STRENGTH. THE STORM WILL NEVER TAKE YOU OUT IF YOU STAY ROOTED AND GROUNDED IN JESUS CHRIST AND HIS LOVE.

Remember what I said earlier about bringing God Glory by standing? My wife and I both believe our ministry in this season of life is to equip people to stand. When we started our podcast, "Anchored with Mike Robinson", which airs on all podcast platforms and Hope Radio, we did it with the intent to help people stay anchored to Jesus and weather any storm.

GROW WHERE GOD PLANTS YOU

I mentioned earlier, that around 30 years ago, we were given a prophetic word about being like an oak tree. This was before we planted the church and before we owned the property with the Grand Champion Oak tree on it. (Just a side note, prophecy should be a confirmation of what God is already speaking to you, not the leading voice in your life. The Word of God is our leading voice).

When we saw the mighty oak tree at the church property, and the fact that it was the only tree on the property, it was a clear confirmation to plant the church in Friendsville, MD. I wanted to go to Morgantown, WV, and plant a church. I wanted to go back to where I was so broken at West Virginia University and help others who were like I used to be. Logically, Morgantown seemed right, it was way bigger and had more opportunities in every way, but God clearly marked out Friendsville, MD. Friendsville is the place of my roots. I was born and raised here, I was born again here, and God had me stay planted here. Even though it went against my human reasoning, I obeyed God and in hindsight, I thank God for planting us here. This church, in this small town, has a worldwide impact. It is an Epicenter for Revival in this region. Anchor Church is, in fact, an anchor here. Fire in the Mountains, now named Fire Brand, is our annual youth conference which has touched and changed hundreds of lives. By standing here for over three decades, we have seen many prayers answered and lives altered and set on fire for God. We have had opportunities to leave and quit. We just never took them. God never released us to leave, so we just keep digging deeper roots into His will. We are still standing.

STILL STANDING AFTER THE STORM

When the tornado came through our town years ago, it took us totally off guard. Talk about a sudden storm. As I drove the two miles from my house to the church, the sky began to change before my eyes. We live in snow country, not tornado country. Tornados are rare. On one side, the sky was beautiful, and on the other side, it was black. When I arrived at the church, my son-in-law Zach was already there. As I shut the truck door, I realized it was the set-up for a tornado. I went in, and Zach was playing on the keyboard. I said, "**It's really weird outside. I think we should go downstairs.**" He said, "**Wait until I get my computer and piano.**" At about the time he ended with the o in piano, it sounded like a train was coming. The church began to shake. The window above the platform blew out, and we ran down to the basement just in time.

When the storm stopped, it suddenly became silent. We looked out the basement window, and from our view, it looked like the mighty oak had fallen. We couldn't believe our eyes, so we slowly went outside to investigate. However, it didn't take the tree, it only took down a huge forty-foot limb that stretched from the tree to the main road.

WE LOOKED AROUND, AND IT TOOK ABOUT A DOZEN OTHER TREES DOWN IN A LINE FOR THE NEXT BLOCK, BUT THE MIGHTY OAK STOOD.

I thought of Psalm 91:7 that says, A thousand shall fall at your side, ten thousand at your right hand, but it will not come near you.

The tree stood the storm. The root system passed. In Luke 6:47-49 (ESV) Jesus talks about our foundation, which is equal to the trees root system. He said,

"Everyone who comes to me and hears my words and does them, I will show you what he is like: he is like a man building a house, who dug deep and laid the foundation

on the rock. And when a flood arose, the stream broke against that house and could not shake it, because it had been well built. But the one who hears and does not do them is like a man who built a house on the ground without a foundation. When the stream broke against it, immediately it fell, and the ruin of that house was great."
Luke 6:47-49 ESV

From this text we can take away several things which apply to the oak tree in the tornado, as well as each of us.

1. It's too late to build a foundation or grow roots in good soil while the storm is raging. If you are hearing God, prepare now, because storms will come. Don't be caught off guard.

2. We have to dig deep to build a good foundation, just like roots have to grow deep to give the tree a good foundation. Two trees or two houses can look the same on the outside, but have a very different foundation.

3. When the storm came, the strength of the foundation and the roots were tested. Notice He says, when the storm comes, not if the storm comes.

BETRAYAL IS ONE STORM IN LIFE.

To me, betrayal is like a tornado in life. It brews as unseen forces are at work, and one day it forms into a major storm.

A betrayal of any kind is painful to the core. It's a break of trust, it's a sucker punch, a knife in the back. It's hard to relate to someone else's betrayal unless you have been there. Whether someone is unfaithful to you, being fired or let go from a job, being undermined, used or abused and manipulated for someone else's gain, it's all hard. As a Christian and a pastor in a small town, I can tell you betrayal is like a tornado, because some pieces can never be put back together. The only thing to do is keep yourself in the love of God, keep free of offense and un-forgiveness, and move on. Once you become bitter, you are done. I have seen people become bitter. I never want that. I can honestly say that what Jesus did in the wilderness by using the Word as absolute truth will keep you on track. I also had to find my identity in Jesus Christ, and not what people think. Only finding your identity in Christ can get you through the pain.

Remember, Jesus had twelve disciples, and one was a betrayer named Judas. Jesus loved him just the same as the others. It's easy to say we love Jesus, but it's harder to love Judas. Staying sweet after betrayal, instead of wanting revenge or closing off to people in general, is a victory. I can say from experience that working through it can be a process. The only reason I believe I can write this today is because I have worked through the betrayals in my life to this point. I have no ax to grind or finger to point.

My family has walked through 4 notable betrayal

tornados while we have been in ministry. We have bent in several directions and have even lost limbs, but our roots have held and we did not break. There were times God had to hold us tight, and we held each other. The Apostle Paul said, "there was a time all forsook him but Jesus". I felt that way, but I had a handful of people that loved me and stood with me no matter what. I am so grateful for that. When Judas betrayed Jesus, it actually got the ball rolling for Jesus to finish the work He was called here to do. What Satan meant for evil, God turned around for good. God still does that for us today.

FOR US AS TREES, THE STORMS CAUSE OUR ROOTS TO DIG IN MORE, AND THE CORE OF OUR BEING BECOMES STRONGER.

I don't have it all figured out, and I am not standing in line to be betrayed, but if it happened to Jesus, it will happen to us. Let me share two of the betrayals we experienced.

BETRAYAL 1

When I first became a Christian and God called me into ministry, I saw the need to have the right Biblical structure in the church. I saw that there are modern day Apostles, and Sandy and I connected to one. It was during the height of something called the "Shepherding Movement", which was really a counterfeit to God's real order in Ephesians 4: 11-15. I have found that many times when you find a truth in scripture, especially in structure and order, that abuses come by people the enemy raises up to muddy the water. When abuses and betrayals come, many are so wounded they never recover. It's why we have so many people who say they love Jesus, but don't want anything to do with church or organized religion. I really understand. People don't lose their faith, they lose hope. They lose hope in other people through betrayal, or even perceived betrayal.

The Apostle we connected to was a false Apostle, and he used manipulation, control, the gift of prophecy or false prophecy in our case, and his personal charisma for his gain. He tried to destroy us, our marriage, the ministry, and our relationship with Christ. This went on for several years. He told me I was no longer anointed and that I should turn the ministry over. When God finally exposed it, we were left wounded and devastated. I didn't think we would recover. I didn't care about ministry. I just wanted to minister to my wife, my daughter, and love Jesus.

I WAS DONE WITH MINISTRY AND DONE WITH THE CHURCH.

In all honesty, I was even afraid I would go back into my old life of partying, because the pain was too great.

We ran away for a weekend to Virginia Beach, VA. It was off season, and cold and rainy. We decided to go to Rock Church, founded by John and Anna Gimenez. I will never forget that day. We were early, and an usher came and began to show us God's love. He looked at my open bible and said, "**You are reading the good stuff!**" He then smiled at me like an angel, and he may have even been one.

The church filled up and worship started. I had my eyes closed, and beside me I could hear a tambourine that really irritated me. It irritated me so much that I just wished it would stop. I opened my eyes and looked over. The lady was burned. And when I say burned, I mean severely. Her face was 100 percent burned, her nose was missing, she had no hair, her right arm had just a stub, and with her burned left arm she played the Tambourine. Beside her were two little children who were also burned. I began to weep. This still makes me weep as I write it. I thought, "**Dear God, if she can praise You, what is wrong with me? Forgive me God. Forgive me for not praising You, forgive me for my self pity, forgive me Jesus for not understanding how much You suffered for me. I should be able to share in a little of Your suffering without quitting. Help me Lord, I am broken.**" I was weeping uncontrollably by this time. By the time worship ended, I was drained and I just sat down.

Then a woman of God named Anna Gimenez walked out on the platform. I never met her, but she pointed at me and said these words, "**You may think you are barely hanging on to God, but the only reason you are here is because He is hanging on to you! You are called by God. Now, go**

back home and do what God called you to do!" I knew that day God loved me so much that even on my worst day, He was there, and He is with you today as you read this.

I found out later that the lady beside me who was burned severly had lost her whole family except her two grandchildren in a fire. God didn't use an apostle to rescue me that day. He used an usher, a burned lady with a tambourine, and a Prophetess to rescue me from my pit.

I went back, and Sandy and I began to pick up the pieces. We had a lot of collateral damage in our lives to deal with. Thank God people like Wayne and Bonnie Stotler, Keith and Darla Collins, and some faithful people from our church were there for us.

I had been betrayed by a false Apostle, but God was not done with the apostolic in my life. A Christian Radio announcer called me and said, "**you have tried those who call themselves Apostle and who are not, you have been faithful to God. God is saying I will give you the real thing and one day you will be the real thing yourself.**"

In prayer one day, the Lord spoke in my heart, "**You have served a Saul as unto me and I will give you a David.**" Shortly after that, in 1999, I heard Apostle John Polis on the radio. He was having a conference for ministers in Elkins, WV, called School of the Shepherds. At that place, God joined my wounded heart to a real servant leader and Apostle. He helped us heal, because it took a long time for us to trust. All he has ever done is serve us for the past twenty-four years.

BETRAYAL 2

On another occasion, as I was praying on day, I knew something was wrong in the church. In my prayer time, everything seemed great, but when I got to church, there was a lack of freedom in that place. I read about John Wesley going on a 40 day bread and water fast and decided to go on one myself. Every day I ate a slice of bread and drank water. It was the most warfare I have ever experienced on a fast. I remember asking God specifically to show me the needle in the haystack. On the fortieth day, I began to see the signs of a storm. Someone on our staff was caught in immorality. We called them into account and removed them from their position, offering restoration. It didn't go well. False information moved like a tornado and tore up a lot. When we assessed the damage, there was a mass exodus from the congregation. Some just left without a word, others told us goodbye. We told our children that people come and people go, but it still hurts.

We got to a place where our Spiritual Father, Dr. John Polis, saw our pain and told us we had two options. He said, **"You can either ride it out and the church will come back, or you can leave and God will bless you somewhere else because you have been faithful."** We prayed and chose to stay, but it was not easy or quick. One of the last families that left had a meeting with us and Dr. John. Before the meeting, Dr. John could see how hurt and fragile we were. He said, "**You know Jesus forgave everyone right there while He was still on the cross.**" That blessed me so much. Sandy and I were both free of the offense. We would do what Jesus did and humble ourselves. Honestly, the meeting felt horrible, but we were able to say, "**Father, forgive them for they know not what they do**." (Luke 22:34)

The next service we had around 10-13 people in church. Down from over 100. We felt like we should just humble ourselves and wash each person's feet. When we finished that night, the storm ended. People still talked, people still gossiped etc..., however we moved on. Reinhard Bonnke said, "**I am on a combine harvester and too busy to get off to catch a mouse.**" We have learned that criticism is just like a bunch of mice. It makes you look for any place in your life they can get in, like a hole in your character. Then after you check your character, keep going. Don't ever stop to catch a mouse, or you could miss a harvest.

> **WE CAN NEVER BE MORE IMPRESSED BY THE DEVIL THAN WE ARE IMPRESSED BY THE FAITHFULNESS OF GOD. HE WILL NEVER LEAVE US NOR FORSAKE US. GOD ALWAYS COMES THROUGH.**

Be like a tree and stand the storm. The storm will end. It will get better. The Bible says in Luke 4:48 that the storm couldn't shake the house. One place it says, the house did not fall because it was built on the rock. Like the tree in Psalm 1:3, you will bare fruit in your season. Be like the tree and stand the storm.

THE WEENIE KING

After the storm, we were not sure financially how we would make it. Sandy and I both have been Bi-vocational during our years of ministry. We have always considered ourselves missionaries to this small town in the wilderness. God has always provided, but we always want to know we are pleasing Him. I have done sales jobs, contracting work, handy-man services, Driving Jobs, etc. This time when I prayed, I really believed I was to buy a Hot Dog cart. What?! Yes, a Hot Dog cart. Sandy laughed, my friends laughed. You must understand, if I didn't have a sense of humor, I wouldn't make it. It's God's gift to me. It did not make sense logically, and it was even humbling to think that a pastor everyone knew in this small town would start selling Hot Dogs. I embraced it, and started studying Hot Dog carts. Did I mention that I really like hot dogs?

My dear friend Keith Collins was in to preach for us, and I told him about what God had shown me. We were driving back to the airport in Pittsburgh, PA, and I said jokingly, **"I'm going to be the weenie king!"** We were laughing so hard, and then like a divine appointment, the Oscar Mayer

Wiener Car passed us going the other way on the interstate. We were amazed! I said, "**that settles it. I don't know why, but I'm going to be the weenie King!**"

One day, about a month later, we were having a yard sale, and a gentleman stopped by. He was going to open a thrift store and asked what I would take for everything? I said, "**One thousand dollars with the chrome wheels I had.**" He said, "**Would you like to make a deal on a Hot Dog cart?**" I could hardly believe my ears. In a small town of 600 people, God brought a stranger with a Hot Dog cart right to our yard sale. What are the chances? I know it doesn't sound Spiritual but there was no doubt God did it. If God could do that, He could restore Sandy and me after this storm. The Hot Dog cart was worth around three thousand dollars. I had $800.00 to my name. That man traded us everything in the yard sale and $800.00 for the cart.

We named the Business "ZuZu Dogs" after our miniature Dachshund. For Two Years that cart helped supplement our income, but more than that, we were able to use it to share the Gospel and pray for people as well. God used it to help restore us and stop the enemy in his tracks. I can't explain it, but I knew if God could bring us that Hot Dog cart and we could reach souls with that, He would restore our church. If I heard God on a Hot Dog cart, then I surely heard God on planting a church.

Lastly, it was like a garden of Gethsemane experience.

We felt all alone. We felt defeated. I didn't understand why we needed a Hot Dog cart, but when I said, "**Not my will, but thine be done**" The victory was won. We would rebuild from the storm, and by the grace of God, we did.

QUESTIONS TO CONSIDER BEFORE THE STORM:

1. Is your foundation firmly on Christ today?

2. If you have been betrayed, is there anyone you need to forgive today?

3. What does Luke 22:34 say?

4. How does Luke 22:34 apply to you?

Chapter 7

PEST AND INSECTS

Pest: insects and animals that are a nuisance to the tree. A pest left unchecked can shorten the life of the tree and even kill it.

In Matthew 26:36-46 we look at the life of Jesus and His time in the Garden of Gethsemane right before His crucifixion. Let's read it:

> "Then Jesus came with them to a place called Gethsemane, and said to the disciples, "Sit here while I go and pray over there." And He took with Him Peter and the two sons of Zebedee, and He began to be sorrowful and deeply distressed. Then He said to them, "My soul is exceedingly sorrowful, even to death. Stay here and watch with Me." He went a little farther and fell on His face, and prayed,

saying, "O My Father, if it is possible, let this cup pass from Me; nevertheless, not as I will, but as You will." Then He came to the disciples and found them sleeping, and said to Peter, "What! Could you not watch with Me one hour? Watch and pray, lest you enter into temptation. The spirit indeed is willing, but the flesh is weak." Again, a second time, He went away and prayed, saying, "O My Father, if this cup cannot pass away from Me unless I drink it, Your will be done." And He came and found them asleep again, for their eyes were heavy. So He left them, went away again, and prayed the third time, saying the same words. Then He came to His disciples and said to them, "Are you still sleeping and resting? Behold, the hour is at hand, and the Son of Man is being betrayed into the hands of sinners. Rise, let us be going. See, My betrayer is at hand." Matthew 26:36-46 NKJV

The pest in our lives are mental battles and spiritual warfare. In the above scriptures, Jesus gives us the ultimate illustration of battle and victory in mental and spiritual warfare.

One day, I was sitting at the picnic table in our yard beside the mighty oak and I noticed a black spot in the grass. I walked over to investigate and saw a trail of ants going through the grass and up the tree into an opening. Those ants came through the yard and up the tree relatively undetected. They entered an opening, or wound, in the tree. This is how pests come in to destroy our lives.

LONLINESS

I believe most people's biggest battle is in the mind. Social media connects the whole world to us, and yet we are the loneliest. It was so sad during the COVID pandemic how many died alone. Many people are sadly isolated in a meta-verse world without meaningful relationships. The suicide rate is alarming. Christians and Non-Christians struggle. I didn't know how lonely life can be, even as a Christian. I believe the struggle with being alone is an opening in our tree. I have dealt with it many times. No one ever told me when I became a Christian that many times you will stand alone in your opinions, alone because you won't sin like others, alone because you differ from the world and alone because you have left old toxic relationships. Being alone as a Christian or minister can be crippling.

In 2 Timothy 4:14-17 the Apostle Paul talks about this to Timothy and us. He says,

> *"Alexander the coppersmith did me much harm, but the Lord will judge him for what he has done. Be careful of him, for he fought against everything we said. The first time I was brought before the judge, no one came with me. Everyone abandoned me. May it not be counted against them. But the Lord stood with me and gave me strength so that I might preach the Good News in its entirety for all the Gentiles to hear. And he rescued me from certain death." 2 Timothy 4:14-17 NLT*

I must admit, I don't believe I have done as well as the Apostle Paul in my times of abandonment.

I KNOW THE LORD WILL NEVER LEAVE US OR FORSAKE US, AND THAT'S THE FACT; HOWEVER, KNOWING AND FEELING ARE TWO DIFFERENT THINGS.

Sandy and I, as ministers, went through a time without close friends. We had to leave our first church. We wanted to move away, but felt we had to stay in our town. Many misunderstood us and we couldn't respond. We were young; we had a 5-year-old, and we didn't do everything right, but we followed God to the best of our ability. During that time, Sandy had a miscarriage. We had no one to understand and tell. We didn't let our family know, so we just held it in. We felt very alone. Stopping at the local store or gas station was difficult due to constant gossip. The enemy came like millions of ants into the open wounds of our tree. They were destroying us from the inside out. One day our dear friend, Pastor Wayne Stotler, told us to join hands, hold our heads high, and walk down main street because we had nothing to be ashamed of. We did that walk down Main Street, and it helped a lot. We firmly declared staying in town as God's calling and refused to be forced out. We must find our identity in walking with the Lord and knowing He will never leave us or forsake us.

The enemy left Jesus in the wilderness, and now at the garden of Gethsemane he comes back camouflaged like the ants I saw in the grass by the oak tree. He said he would return at an opportune time, and he did. Three disciples failed to comprehend Jesus' struggle. They didn't understand the way He operated. He even told them, my soul is sorrowful to the point of death, but they didn't respond. The disciple John had placed his head on the chest of Jesus. This helped me, because I can see that John was so close to Jesus, but He couldn't see the struggle. He didn't realize the enormous pressure Jesus was facing, or the attack against Him spiritually and emotionally. I have felt like the closest people to me could not understand me before, and I don't hold it against them, but it motivates me to want to notice need in others. I pray we are never too busy to notice when someone feels alone.

One time I was at a ministers' conference and a severe storm hit. The power was out in the motel, and only certain restaurants in the area with generator power were serving food. As I walked through the dark lobby of the motel, I saw a minister I had only met one time. He was sitting on a sofa in the lobby by himself. I asked him to go have dinner with us, and he agreed. We enjoyed our conversation and returned to the conference. We talked most of the weekend. When I returned home, I received an email from this man. He told me he had gone there discouraged and intended on taking his life in the motel. He felt like a failure in all roles - husband, provider, and pastor. He just had the thought in the lobby before I came by that nobody even noticed him or cared. Then I stopped by. He said that dinner saved his life, and he wanted to thank God and me. I never prayed with him, I never shared scriptures that I remember, I just shared dinner with him. I understand loneliness in ministry and as a Christian. I have such a heart for ministers and their families. This man made me realize that a small act of kindness during someone's loneliness can create a significant change.

I would never have guessed he was there to take His life. I am sure if one of his family members or church members would have seen him in the motel lobby, they wouldn't have picked up on it. It helped me to relate to Jesus' disciples.

The disciples with Jesus in the Garden just didn't get it. Jesus comes back after asking them to pray, and they are asleep. What? He wakes them and says, "**couldn't you pray with me for one hour?**" Jesus prays three times and the disciples never do get it.

This is what blesses me. They wouldn't stand with Him, but He never stopped loving them. His identity was not in them, it was in the Father. In His humanity, I'm sure He felt alone and let down by them, but He didn't get mad at them. He felt sorry for them. He said, "**Let's go. It's time for me to be betrayed.**" I admit many times I have been upset as a young Christian and pastor at people who stop at some point in their walk and go to sleep. The greatest thing we can do is feel sorry for them and pray for them. We must love them and move on. This closes up the hole for the ants in our tree, so to speak. Then the pests and insects can't get in. This stops any rot and decay on the inside. Trees are like people in that they can look good on the outside, but be rotting on the inside.

The Bible says, Confess your faults, that you may be healed. I found out the opposite is also true. When we don't confess our faults, we can become sick inside. When we try to go it alone without God and battle within ourselves, the war intensifies. Any area of darkness or struggle we withhold from God is a place for the enemy to feed on. I always say the enemy is like a Mud Sucker fish. He is a bottom feeder. He goes after the things we hide inside. It's like those ants going into that opening on the tree and slowly eating and making a home in the tree. The tree looks ok on the outside, but it's slowly being destroyed. Jesus gave us an example of how to take the enemy head on.

When Jesus said, "**Not my will but thine be done**", He was submitting to God, resisting His flesh and the Devil, and stopping the pest in its tracks. Jesus was drawing a line with the enemy by using God's Word. When we submit to God and resist the Devil, He has to run away from us (James 4:7-8). It's just like in Matthew 4, where Jesus says, "**If anyone will follow me, they must deny themselves and take up their cross and follow me.**"

I heard Benny Hinn say one time, "**The more light you have, the more bugs you will draw**"

The Word of God is an organic bug killer.

I believe Jesus won the victory in the Garden before He ever went to the cross. That line He drew, and that stand He made, gave Him what he needed to finish what the Father had commissioned Him to do.

I believe today that God is going to give you victory in your garden of loneliness and despair. How the enemy meant to quietly destroy you is being exposed today. This will prepare you for your destiny on the other side of this wilderness.

QUESTIONS TO CONSIDER:

1. Is there an area inside that's destroying you that you need to confess and get help? (please reach out today) James 5:16 says, "Confess your trespasses to one another, and pray for one another, that you may be healed. The effective, fervent prayer of a righteous man avails much." Confessing our faults and letting someone in we can trust will bring healing. Find someone and reach out. No one warned me about the loneliness in the wilderness, but thank God I finally got help.

2. Is there someone you need to support in prayer like

the disciples should have supported Jesus? (Maybe a leader or pastor in your life. Make it a point to pray confidentially for leaders in your life.)

3. Is there someone you need to reach out to that seems all alone?

Chapter 8

FOREST FIRE

Fire: a state, process, or instance of combustion in which fuel or other material is ignited and combined with oxygen, giving off light, heat and flame. (dictionary.com)

Wildfires in the wilderness can burn out of control and do catastrophic damage to the forest and wildlife. The same destructive fire that destroys also purifies.

A CONTROLLED BURN

When I was about ten years old, I remember going to South Carolina. As we were traveling, the traffic came to a halt. I remember seeing road crews and smoke along the road. I leaned up from the back seat and said, "**Look dad, it's a forest fire!**" To which he replied, "**Don't worry, it's a**

controlled burn." I had never seen a controlled burn in our small town of Friendsville, MD. My dad explained to me that a controlled burn, and even a forest fire, can be a good thing. I learned it burns the underbrush, replenishes the soil, kills disease and pests that kill trees, and it actually makes the way for the forest to continue for generations. Fire in the wilderness is necessary for growth.

> **FIRE BRINGS PURIFICATION, NEW GROWTH, AND LIFE.**

God is the one who uses fire like a controlled burn in our lives to bring purification. He calls it the trying of our faith. Every tree must go through the fire at some point.

RUN TO THE FIRE

To further illustrate this point, I was having communion one morning with the Lord and He said, "**Gold doesn't run from the fire of purification!**" Wow, I was taken aback by that thought. Instead of running from the fire, or praying for it to stop, I needed to go through it. Fire and purification are not only necessary for the forest, they are necessary for you and I.

In 1 Peter 3:3-7 it states;

> *"Blessed be the God and Father of our Lord Jesus Christ, who according to His abundant mercy has begotten us again to a living hope through the resurrection of Jesus Christ from the dead, to an inheritance incorruptible*

and undefiled and that does not fade away, reserved in heaven for you, who are kept by the power of God through faith for salvation ready to be revealed in the last time. In this you greatly rejoice, though now for a little while, if need be, you have been grieved by various trials, that the genuineness of your faith, being much more precious than gold that perishes, though it is tested by fire, may be found to praise, honor, and glory at the revelation of Jesus Christ." 1 Peter 3:3-7 NKJV

Fire doesn't just try us emotionally, physically, and spiritually. It tries our motives. Notice in the above scripture that it's not our faith that is more valuable than gold it's the genuineness of our faith. People look at the outward appearance, but God looks at the heart. God looks at the core and authenticity of our faith. God wants to purify, cleanse, and shake us from the depths of our being so we can shake the nations of this world. We can see around the world that God is purifying and exposing sin among church leaders and churches. He is coming back for a glorious church. His glorious church will be a church that has been purified by fire.

HIS GLORIOUS CHURCH WILL LIVE FROM A PURE MOTIVE. WE WILL LIVE FOR HIS PRAISE, HIS HONOR, AND HIS GLORY, NOT OUR OWN.

Society changes daily before our eyes. We are getting a front-row seat of post-modernism at work. Values have changed, morals have changed, ideals have changed, sermons have changed, churches have changed, but God has not changed.

God has not been taken off guard, nor is He shaken by any of this. He is divinely carrying out His plan through those who will hear and obey His voice. He is searching the whole earth and looking for those in the wilderness that He can show Himself strong through. In 2 Chronicles 16:9, we can see the eyes of the Lord searching the whole earth in order to strengthen those whose hearts are fully committed to Him. God will flex His strength only through those who have been purified by Fire! He is raising up Five-Fold ministers right now. He is bringing a troop of modern day Apostles, Prophets, Pastors, Teachers and Evangelists who are true sent ones and shepherds to His flock. God shows us a glimpse in Jeremiah 3:15 when He says, "**I will give you shepherds after my own heart, who will feed you with knowledge and understanding.**" Those with His heart will only be those who have been through the Fire. God will not share His true glory with self proclaimed, self appointed and self anointed Hollywood types. Promotion comes from the Lord. Before God promotes us and sends us, we must be purified. Before God sends us, He wants to cleanse us! The vision Isaiah had in Isaiah 6:1-7 illustrates my point.

"In the year that King Uzziah died, I saw the Lord, high

and exalted, seated on a throne; and the train of his robe filled the temple. Above him were seraphim, each with six wings: With two wings they covered their faces, with two they covered their feet, and with two they were flying. And they were calling to one another: "Holy, holy, holy is the Lord Almighty; the whole earth is full of his glory." At the sound of their voices the doorposts and thresholds shook and the temple was filled with smoke. "Woe to me!" I cried. "I am ruined! For I am a man of unclean lips, and I live among a people of unclean lips, and my eyes have seen the King, the Lord Almighty." Then one of the seraphim flew to me with a live coal in his hand, which he had taken with tongs from the altar. With it he touched my mouth and said, "See, this has touched your lips; your guilt is taken away and your sin atoned for." Isaiah 6:1-7 NIV

Isaiah's ministry went from a "Woe is you ministry" to a "Woe is me ministry." In the first five chapters, Isaiah is pointing the finger at others, but in Isaiah chapter six, he has a purifying encounter with the purifying fire of God!

The burning of his lips changed his words. I believe it signified the burning up of his old ways, his old wounds, his old wine skin, his old paradigms, and his old strategies. Fire purified everything.

THE PURPOSE OF THE FIRE

God wants to purify us in the fire on our wilderness

journey so He will have a people who are transformed into the image of Christ. The fire of God is transformational. Just like Isaiah was transformed by his encounter with fire, we will be transformed as well.

I believe God's overall purpose for the controlled burn in the wilderness is to purify three things. He wants to purify the messenger, the message, and the methods the church uses to get us back to the book of Acts in the Bible. We see fire also recorded in the book of Acts when tongues of fire rested on each person. Instead of tongs with a coal on one person, tongues of fire fell on every person. That same transformational fire is for every believer today.

BEAUTY FOR ASHES

The first thing God wants to do is to purify the messenger. As I wrote this chapter, the Lord placed this nugget of encouragement on my heart from Isaiah 61:1-3. "From the altar of death to self come the ashes I will form your beauty from." The NKJV says it like this,

> *"To all who mourn in Israel, he will give a crown of beauty for ashes, a joyous blessing instead of mourning, festive praise instead of despair. In their righteousness, they will be like great oaks that the Lord has planted for his own glory." Isaiah 61:3 NKJV*

This one nugget really made me weep. I have told many people that God will give them beauty for ashes; however, in the midst of the wilderness it's easy to forget that truth. It's especially easy to forget when the fire is raging in your life and it seems as though all is lost.

I looked at the remains of an old shed I had to burn up one day. When I cleaned up the remains, I saw nails, metal door hinges, wire, and ashes. I had the realization that only God could take these ashes and make a new building out of them. It's true for you and me today. Only God could take our burned up lives and make something beautiful again. Be encouraged that wherever the fire comes from in the wilderness, whether it is God's controlled burn or a wildfire of the enemy to destroy us, God will always give us beauty for ashes.

The fire in the wilderness takes us to the Throne Of Grace, where we have no other choice but to trust God. Purification in our lives makes more room for God. The more purification in us, the more glory God will receive through it! This is not a martyr mentality. It is just a by-product of the consuming fire of God in our lives. God increases and we decrease. Purification takes us on a path from the outer court, to the inner court, to the Holy place.

FIVE THINGS TO KNOW ABOUT PERSONAL PURIFICATION:

The first thing to know about personal purification is that it's maintained by communion with God. Communion means relationship, partnership, and fellowship. These all describe prayer. Prayer is our oxygen in the fire. It sustains us.

The second thing to know about personal purification is that stewardship is involved. We must steward our time, our mind, and our mouth to increase an awareness of Him. In this realm of prayer and stewardship, we learn what grieves God as well as what pleases Him. This creates intimacy with Him. True intimacy with God is when prayer becomes a love affair.

The third thing about personal purification is that it is maintained through genuine worship in spirit and in truth (John 4:24).

The fourth thing about personal purification is that you can not rebuke it. You can rebuke the devil and he will flee, but you can not rebuke the trying of your faith. It is a must for gold to go through the fire.

The fifth thing, and the end result of purification, is that we come out it of gold.

Gold is the goal of the fire in our wilderness. I encourage you to go for the Gold. Do not quit because there is a finish line. There is a way out of the wilderness, and when you look back at life, and forward to eternity, you will know it was worth it. In essence, Proverbs 17:3 in my translation says silver and gold are tested by flames of fire and our thoughts and motives are tested by the Lord. We may be tempted to run out of the fire at times; however, when we see Jesus, and we hear Him say, "**Well Done!**" It will be worth it after all!

QUESTIONS TO CONSIDER ABOUT THE FIRES IN YOUR LIFE:

1. Where is the fire coming from in my life today? Is it the trying of my faith, or is this a demonic spiritual attack? Or perhaps a result of sin in my life? Note: Once we answer this question, we know what to do next. It is:

   A. Walk on through the controlled burn (1 Peter 3:3-7).

   B. Take authority over the spiritual attack by submitting to God, resisting the devil and seeing him flee (James 4:7).

   C. Repenting of sin and receive the refreshing in the wilderness (Acts 3:19).

2. Are you willing to trust God in the fire?

3. To maintain your personal purification, which area needs the most attention? Communion and prayer, stewardship or worship?

4. Will you make a commitment to go for the gold today?

Chapter 9

SICKNESS AND DISEASE:

During my research for this book, I discovered something incredibly fascinating about tree sickness and disease. According to the University of Arkansas Division of Agriculture, Common Tree Disease problems are cankers. Cankers are areas of dead bark and underlying wood on twigs, branches, and the trunk. The many fungi that cause cankers normally inhabit the surface of the tree. It's interesting that the fungi enter through natural or man-made wounds, and only cause disease when the tree is under stress.

HUMANS VS. TREES

The more I see the comparison between us and trees, the more I see how big God is! God is the Creator of all things, and I don't want to get off track in this chapter, but all creation praises Him.

> "All the earth bows down to you; they sing praise to you, they sing the praises of your name." Psalm 66:4 NIV

And the more we study nature, the more we can see God as the Creator. When God says to be like a tree, and we really dig into it, the comparison is mind-blowing. We were meant to live in perfect health forever, but then sin came in through Satan to ruin that.

A tree is meant to live on and on, but wounds that come from the natural fallen environment and from man cause disease and sickness to infect trees. It's interesting also that trees are most vulnerable to sickness under stress, and so are we.

Here is the Good news. Jesus came to intervene for us! According to Isaiah 53:4-5, Jesus has borne our griefs (sicknesses, weaknesses, and distresses) and He carried our sorrows and pains (of punishment). He was wounded for our transgressions; He was bruised for our guilt and sin. The chastisement for us to obtain peace and wellbeing was upon Him, and by the stripes made from whipping HIM on His back, WE are healed and made whole. I learned to put my name in Isaiah 53:4-5 as I read it out loud, and it becomes Faith building. Let's try it together now,

*Surely He has borne **our** (your name) griefs And carried **our** (your name)sorrows; Yet **we** (your name) esteemed Him stricken, Smitten by God, and afflicted. But He was wounded for **our** (your name) transgressions, He was bruised for **our** (your name) iniquities; The chastisement for **our** (your name) peace was upon Him, and by His stripes **we** (your name) are healed. Isaiah 53:4-5 NKJV*

Of all things, Jesus was crucified on a cross, but the Bible refers to it as a tree! Galatians 3:13 (my paraphrase) says, Jesus Christ rescued us from the curse of the law, which is sin, sickness and spiritual death. When He was hung on the cross, He took upon Himself the curse for our wrongdoing. It is written in the Bible. Cursed is everyone who is hung on a tree.

They tortured and crucified Jesus on a cross for our sin and our sicknesses and diseases. Sickness and disease will not only stop a tree and a Christian from growing, it will kill us both.

For the next portion of this chapter, I would like to share some of the struggles that not only I faced, but also my family faced, and how God through it all is still faithful

NO MORE SURGERY

Like many people, I have faced attacks of sickness and disease, but I have also experienced miracles and healing.

From conception, Psalm 118:17 has been true in my life. I would not die but live and declare the works of the Lord.

I mentioned my birth story earlier and how miraculous it was; however, there's more. At age 40, and while Sandy was eight months pregnant, my appendix burst. I waited 8 days to go to the hospital. They operated, and I was full of infection. Six days later, I was still not improving because of a bowel obstruction. I remember my dad's face as he talked to the surgeon in the hallway outside my room. Dad said, "**He will not make it, is he?**" I could see my dad's head shaking No from my bed. I was at a low point. One day later, they operated again. I was so weak my heart stopped briefly at the end of the surgery. I went into intensive care for six more days. Then the bowel obstructed again.

> **IN THE HOSPITAL CHAPEL, MY WIFE SANDY DECLARED, "NO MORE SURGERY!" THE LORD HAD SPOKEN, NO MORE SURGERY. SEVENTY-TWO HOURS LATER, I WAS DOING BETTER.**

The Dr. did not understand, but we knew God had done it! Twenty-one days after it started, the hospital released me. Shortly after, when I was eating, I had a gall bladder attack that sent me back to the hospital. They wanted to operate on it, but again, no more surgery. I still have my gall bladder.

THE STORY NO ONE KNEW

I have been hesitant to share my latest healing, because

it's still in the process of complete manifestation. Today, I sense a release from God for this book.

Because my family and I have experienced long-term illness, I can relate to people here who are battling sickness and disease. Long-term illness affects the individual battling, as well as the caregivers, friends, and family around them.

Until this past year, I hadn't realized how much my family had gone through in the last eight years. It put so much pressure on my wife and daughter at home that they were at the point of breaking many days. I came to find out that they not only waited on me, prayed for me, and watched my pain, but they experienced their own. In fact, many times they stayed up after I went to bed and cried secretly.

My wife prayed, studied, and stood in faith. She stayed up many nights and prayed until she fell asleep on the sofa, too tired to come to bed. She fasted for me every Monday and enlisted others to do the same.

She helped me get up; she changed our diet; she researched and purchased supplements; she advocated with doctors and researched hospitals and clinics, and she prayed more about it. There were no fun nights or vacations away. I went from driving everywhere we went to her driving us.

She did 95% of everything, and still helped others, cooked meals for others and the youth of our church and, etc.............

And she never complained or spoke negatively! Not even one time I know of. We had to trust God every day and in every way. Spiritually, emotionally, physically, and financially.

My youngest daughter felt so helpless and trapped. She knew that our faith was at the point that we didn't tell people what we were going through. We didn't want pity, or for gossip to spread about how sick I was, so she held it in too. The painful thing was, she herself had no one to confide in and pray with. I missed it big time with her. I should have been more sensitive to her pain. After all, I am the dad. There is no condemnation on me now about this, but it really hit me hard at first. I tell this part of the story to help others, because it could have damaged my daughter and her walk with God. I should have been more sensitive to my family's needs. Being in pain everyday put me in a bubble of survival, and I didn't realize how much I had changed. I didn't realize how different my words and actions came across to my family. I learned something. When one suffers pain in the family, we all suffer pain.

Then it fell on my oldest daughter Tabitha and my son-in-law Zach, as well as my closest friends: Keith, Mags, Ken and Joe, and my closest spiritual sons and daughters. It went all down the line to the church.... I hid it well from people who didn't know me as well, but those closest to me went through it with me. I felt helpless and frustrated many times. I struggled. I would get very upset as I laid in bed, and they went for walks and had talks. I could see them having a life without me. The enemy was right there in my ear, telling me, "**This is what it will be like when you are gone.**"

Besides the chronic pain, I dealt with guilt and discouragement.

I thank God we could get health insurance, but still we had all the bills, the special foods, the gas money …. it cost so much. One year we had paid our $5,400 deductible, and then the insurance company moved out of our state. We then had to start all over again and pay the full deductible to the next company. For us, that might as well have been $54,000! The devil really tried me with this. I battled guilt for robbing my family. At the same time, God used several precious people to send money. Some paid for motel rooms at the Cleveland clinic. My dad gave us unexpected money for food, and people handed us money for gas. One friend started buying me 2 supplements every month and on and on. One store gave me a discount on all supplements, and people brought us food. Every single gift and every single word of encouragement, and especially every prayer, meant so much.

ONE BRIEF WORD CAN BE LIKE BREATH TO A SUFFOCATING PERSON, BECAUSE YOU CAN FEEL FORGOTTEN.

My best friend Keith called me, prayed for me, and even rented a car to drive 450 miles to my house, then drove me another 230 miles to Cleveland, Ohio, and back for an appointment. People on our team prayed for us, cared for us, and helped at the church and the house. They became Aaron and Hur to us to hold up our hands. Our dear friends Mags and Joe fought hell with us in spiritual warfare over my life! My friend Gordon checked on me constantly. While others walked out of our lives, God used special people to walk in and hold us up.

My heart is filled with compassion for anyone and any caregivers who are facing a battle with sickness and disease. Whether it's been COVID, or cancer, or even a rare autoimmune disease, it's an intense fight. The longer it lasts, the more discouraging it can be.

This is not a formula, it's a piece of my story for God's glory and is like a puzzle that only God could put together. Like my father in the faith, Dr. John Polis says, "**We don't deny sickness, we DEFY sickness!**" My faith had to get more real than ever.

MY HEALING STORY FOR GOD'S GLORY

I want to be transparent with you so you realize you can make it as well. Some people make faith about how strong they are and even look down on others for not having "enough" faith. It's not right. Another thing that hurts people is acting like because of their faith, they never have a problem, but that gives the wrong impression.

I don't know everything, but I believe my story can help you. My wife Sandy said the most profound thing, "**This whole testimony is not just about what God has done, It's about who He is!**" He is Lord, He is Savior, He is the Everlasting Father, He is our Comforter, He is the Prince of Peace, He is King of Kings and Lord of Lords. He is our Healer. He is faithful to us and His word. He is knowable. In fact, He is the great I AM. Psalm 46:1 says, "He is a very present help in time of need." That means when we are in the most need, He is the most near!

In one of Sandy's greatest times of need during this season, the Lord spoke to her heart, "**Your decision to believe Me has set up an impenetrable wall against the enemy.**"

The Word of God is our foundation for life and healing. Throughout this journey we have stood on several scriptures, and without God's Word we would be sunk. I would listen to the scriptures. I would read the scriptures. Sandy would read the Scriptures over me. I would listen to podcasts on healing by John Polis, Charles Capps, Kenneth Hagin, Kenneth Copeland, Jerry Savelle, and Keith Moore. My daily journal became like a trusted friend. One I could pour out my deepest thoughts to. I felt so unable to speak to anyone but Jesus, so I wrote in my journal. On September 23, 2019, I wrote this:

My journal on 9/23/19 up at 4:10am

> *This is what the Good fight of faith is for me right now....*
>
> - *When I wake up, I pray*
> - *When I can't sleep, I take communion*
> - *When I can't move I listen to the Word and Podcasts*
> - *When I can't walk, I sit*
> - *When I can't work with my hands, I read the word and write*
> - *When I can't stay awake, I take a nap.*
> - *When I am in pain, I take my Gos-pills (30 healing scriptures marked in my Bible); I speak out loud to my body to line up with God's Word. I command sickness to go from me and call healing to come to me. I have taken pain pills, but I hate it. Sometimes the pain is so great tears come to my eyes and out of frustration, I cry.*
> - *When I Breakdown, I don't stay down! (Out of the last 3 years, I have had 20 breakdowns but THATS 1,075 days I did not breakdown!!!! Praise God! Praise God! Praise God!)*
>
> *This morning I will just Praise God ..... I am thankful for another day....... END OF Journal ENTRY*

The journals and notebooks I have filled up are valuable

to me. One passage of scripture comes up over and over throughout my journals, and it's Mark 5:25-34. This is known as the woman with the issue of blood.

THE ISSUE OF BLOOD

The woman with the issue of blood and I have much in common. I battled a rare form of vasculitis, an autoimmune disease, and one where blood vessels burst anywhere at any time. This woman in Mark 5 suffered for 12 years with her issue of blood and on top of that had suffered many things from many physicians and had spent all that she had. It didn't get better, but grew worse. I could relate to this story, and it popped up repeatedly throughout my journey.

Today, if you are in the middle of your journey, or you are walking with someone who is, be encouraged! I know it's very taxing to have some doctors who don't treat you like you are going to get well, to have healthcare workers who make mistakes, to have tests and appointments all the time, to have treatments such as chemo and feel worse, to run up your credit card, to spend money that could buy other necessities for your family or put a child through college, to feel like no one understands, to pray and do everything you know to do and feel worse. It can feel hopeless.

A FALLING STAR

Remember my birth story and the star that fell when

I was born? One night, my wife was struggling with me being sick. She said she knew the story about a star falling from the sky when I was born and she needed hope. Just then, a star fell from the sky. My daughter Anna was praying two weeks after that and was crying over me. The reality hit her that I was dying. She said a star fell from the sky in front of her and she knew I would be alright. Just now 11/18/23 at 7pm, as I was typing this, my phone rang and my daughter called and said she was praying in despair for herself and a star fell from the sky! Wow, just wow! God is so good to meet us where we are at.

IT'S A MIRACLE

One day, the Doctor looked at me and said, "**You will never get better!**", then he said, "**without a miracle you will never get better!**" At that point, on that day, it felt like a punch in the gut. But listen, Jesus Christ is the Great Physician! That same doctor (who we love, and God used) would end up saying with excitement, "**It's a miracle, why can't we just call it a miracle? No one says we can't call it a miracle. It's a miracle!**"

THE TOUCH AND THE TRIAL

During the first year, they tested my kidneys, heart and lungs several times for hemorrhaging. Sores would break out on my legs and arms, I would have itching and constant sinus drainage, my blood pressure was out of control, I had shortness of breath, a burning tongue and burning eyes. In July 2018, we were on a trip to Hendersonville, NC, to a ministers' conference, and the vessels in my eyes bled and I was bleeding behind my eye sockets. Driving down, my eyes became worse, and I had cloudy vision. When I went to the conference, Dr. John Polis, my father in the Faith, laid hands on me and prayed. It was like electricity went through my arms and immediately my eyes stopped burning, my vision cleared, and all the blood left my eyes. The whites of my eyes were white again. Praise GOD!

I thought it was all over; however, the other symptoms persisted. It became a fight of faith. A life or death fight of faith.

Then fast forward to June 2019. My Blood Pressure went up to 240/140, and I was short of breath and very weak. I was hospitalized, and even with IV meds, my BP didn't drop. Early the next morning, I asked the nurses to leave me alone for an hour while I prayed and praised God out loud. When I was finished, my BP came down. Later that day, I was released from the hospital.

Throughout all of these sicknesses and diseases, one of the things I have learned is we must own our faith. Smith Wigglesworth had one of a kind of faith. Mike Robinson has his and you have yours. For the remainder of this chapter I want to share, the four greatest things I learned about faith, when the storm doesn't cease and you grow weak in your flesh

THE FOUR GREATEST THINGS I LEARNED ABOUT FAITH

1. Do not quit (QUITTING IS NOT AN OPTION).

2. Do not keep silent (you must speak to it ... maybe thousands of times or more!) 2 Corinthians. 4:16 - We believe and therefore we speak.

   - One day I was wondering if I would ever be able to stand consitently in faith and I said, **"God I don't know if I will ever get this faith thing right. It looks like an EKG ... up and down and up and down!"** God responded to me, **"at least it's not a flat line!"**

3. When we are sinking in our faith like Peter walking on the water, it's alright to pull the ripcord and cry out for mercy! — I mean, let's get real ...

   - Some Christians and 5 fold ministry would rather drown acting like they know everything than pull the ripcord. Sometimes we need to cry our for mercy, and let Jesus rescue us like a child and then allow Him to teach us how to walk and not sink. Don't drown in your imperfect faith, pull the rip cord and then figure it out.

- Pulling the rip cord might be taking treatments you don't want to take, or going to doctors you don't want to go to!

4. We look to Jesus for faith, not inside!

- We BUILD faith on the inside by daily reading and putting the Word of God in our hearts... but we don't LOOK INSIDE for faith, we LOOK TO Jesus. Hebrews 12:2 NKJV says, "looking unto Jesus, the author and finisher of our faith." We don't receive it just because we believe it! We receive it because we believe Him.

- Looking inside becomes a **self help** mentality, or a **look how I did it** mentality. Look how strong I am ... No, we only need to show ourself strong to the devil, to demonically inspired words spoken by people or demonically inspired thoughts that come against us.

Sandy is right, "**My testimony is not about what I have done, or even what Jesus has done! It's about who He is!**" He is the Lord my Healer; He is my Deliverer in the midst of the storm! My Deliverer from COVID, from the fear of COVID, from cancer, from rare diseases, from autoimmune, or from this wicked and perverse generation! My God is so good, and I am so thankful!

December 14th, 2022, the specialist from Cleveland Clinic looked me and Sandy in the eyes and prophesided! She said, "**It's been a long haul for you, but I'm taking this disease off your chart!**" Then she said, "**Go and live your life, you no longer have to worry about dying everyday. MERRY CHRISTMAS!**"

Then our local physician, who had previously claimed that I could never be healed of this, exclaimed, "**Let's call it a miracle...**"

Praise God! Praise God for your miracle today! I tell everyone if I was a cat and had 9 lives, I would give every single one to Jesus. I tell them this not because of what He has done, but because of who He is.

Instead of questions to consider at the end of this chapter, I want you to go over the four things I personally learned about faith and try to incorporate them into your daily life. This will equip you to be ready when the wilderness trial comes.

1. Don't Quit! (Rest if you must, but never quit)

2. Do not keep silent.

3. When you are sinking, pull the ripcord.

4. Keep your eyes on Jesus! (Look to Jesus for your faith, not yourself)

Section 3

COMING OUT OF THE WILDERNESS

MIKE ROBINSON

Chapter 10

LEARNING TO COUNT IN THE WILDERNESS

I know this sounds odd for a 60-year-old man, but I finally learned to count in the thickest wilderness of my life. To make it clear, I am not talking about counting numbers; I am talking about learning to count it all joy. The Bible says in James 1:2-3;

> *"My brethren, count it all joy when you fall into various trials, knowing that the testing of your faith produces patience." James 1:2-3 NKJV*

I must admit that I had struggled with this scripture many times. During this past wilderness season, I spent a lot of time in a lift chair. Not a Chair Lift at a ski resort, but a lift chair in my living room. A lift chair works by electric. It assists you in getting up from the chair and back down in the chair when you are too weak to do it yourself. I journaled every day in that chair. I call this time of journaling "**Life lessons from a lift chair.**" It was in that lift chair that I finally learned to count.

I started a personal Bible study of the book of James. Some people call the Book of James the New Testament book of proverbs. James is not a book on how to become a Christian, it's a book on how to act and behave like a Christian.

In John Maxwell's leadership Bible, his intro to James says, **"James is the book you ought to read standing up. It contains a ringing call for action, a plea for vital Christianity and a faith that shows itself not in mere words but in lifestyle! James is one of the most practical books in the Bible. It teaches that faith without corresponding action is dead."**

I agree with John Maxwell, we should read it standing up, but even when I was laying down, God spoke to me through it and He taught me how to count.

When I read, "Count it all joy when you fall into various trials, knowing that the testing of your faith produces patience." I honestly thought, HOW?! What does that mean? I studied and prayed and meditated in this verse. In my findings, I believe I found a survival tool for the wilderness. The survival tool is learning to count God's way, and from God's perspective.

The term, "Count it all joy" seems simple on the surface; however, what does it mean and how do we do that? I found a key in the Strong's concordance looking up the term, "Count it." The Strong's number is 2230 and, in the one sense, it means to consider, deem, account and think.

From this we can see that the Bible is not saying we should jump around in the wilderness trials of life and say, "Oh Joy!" We shouldn't just continue on in pain like nothing happened. That would be crazy. Pain is pain, not joy. Trials are trials, not sources of pleasure. God doesn't expect us to call pain our joy. That's weird. We call pain what it is, it's pain. God must teach us to count, to consider, to deem, and to think His way instead of with our human reasoning.

2 Corinthians 10:4-6 states;

> *"We use God's mighty weapons, not worldly weapons, to knock down the strongholds of human reasoning and to destroy false arguments. We destroy every proud obstacle that keeps people from knowing God. We capture their rebellious thoughts and teach them to obey Christ. And after you have become fully obedient, we will punish everyone who remains disobedient." 2 Corinthians 10:4-6 NLT*

For the second key of counting it all joy, we must go back to James, chapter one and verse three. This verse states:

"Knowing that the testing of your faith produces patience." James 1:3 NKJV

The word "knowing" is key.

> **WE MUST KNOW JESUS INTIMATELY AND CHOOSE TO BELIEVE HIS WORD IN THE WILDERNESS TRIALS OF OUR LIFE.**

As we walk with the Lord, I believe our knowing is progressive. The Bible says in John 17:3, "To know Him is eternal life." When we first trust Christ as our Lord and Savior, that is our introduction to knowing Him. Then later on, as we walk with Him, we learn more truth, and the truth we learn makes us free. John 8:32 says, "You shall know the truth and the truth shall make you free." Freedom most definitely comes in an instant; however, it also most definitely comes as we get to know the Lord intimately.

The more we walk with the Lord, the more we trust Him. It's like walking with a close friend. I have had a few friends in life that I could trust with anything I have and own. Jesus is a friend that sticks closer than a brother, and knowing Him is key in learning to count it all joy. Over the years of prayer, reading His Word, and experiencing life together, we learn His nature, His character and we learn we can trust Him, no matter what. He is our ultimate guide in the wilderness. Throughout life with Him, we learn that on the darkest days to trust Him. Knowing Him brings us through the hardest times we will ever encounter in life.

EVEN WHEN I DON'T UNDERSTAND

One day in my lift chair I was so broken, I felt weak, fatigued, drained, dry and a million miles from God. I wept before the Lord and I had a "Knowing" moment which likened to counting it all joy.

I sat in the chair, I took communion and I believe the Holy Spirit gave me this thought, "**If I tell others I am a Christ follower and I know Him, then the highest form of knowing Him is to trust Him when I don't understand.**"

We can all trust God when it's easy, and when we can understand what's going on. That doesn't take any faith.

I realized that when I totally surrendered my life to Christ in the wilderness; I surrendered everything I couldn't figure out, and everything I didn't understand. I just have to trust. We will all get into discouragement and hopelessness if we spend our time trying to figure things out, focusing on what didn't go right and what didn't happen, instead of focusing on all the good things that happen and the Goodness of God.

This knowing moment changed ME, not my situation!

It's in this knowing moment that I saw how to count it all with joy. Scriptures flooded my heart like...

"For this light, momentary affliction, is preparing for us an eternal weight of glory beyond all comparison." 2 Corinthians 4:17 ESV

"For I consider that the sufferings of this present time are not worth comparing with the glory that is to be revealed to us." Romans 8:18 ESV

"And we know that for those who love God, all things work together for good, for those who are called according to his purpose." Romans 8:28 ESV

"Rejoice and be glad, for your reward is great in heaven, for so they persecuted the prophets who were before you." Matthew 5:12 ESV

Then the icing on the cake is Romans 8:31-39, which states;

"What then shall we say to these things? If God is for us, who can be against us? He who did not spare his own Son but gave him up for us all. How will he not also with him graciously give us all things? Who shall bring any charge against God's elect? It is God who justifies. Who is to condemn? Christ Jesus is the one who died–more than that, who was raised–who is at the right hand of God, who indeed is interceding for us. Who shall

separate us from the love of Christ? Shall tribulation, or distress, or persecution, or famine, or nakedness, or danger, or sword? As it is written, "For your sake, we are being killed all the day long; we are regarded as sheep to be slaughtered." No, in all these things we are more than conquerors through him who loved us. For I am sure that neither death nor life, nor angels nor rulers, nor things present nor things to come, nor powers, nor height nor depth, nor anything else in all creation, will separate us from the love of God in Christ Jesus our Lord." Romans 8:31-39 ESV

THE POWER OF NOTHING

I call these verses "The power of nothing." Nothing can separate us from God's love! Death can't do it, demons can't do it, principalities can't do it, present problems can't do it. In fact, anything that could ever happen can't do it! Nothing can separate us from the love of God. NO-THING. Nothing. That's the power of nothing!

PAUL HAD TROUBLES TOO

I read all these Scriptures, and the Apostle Paul penned all but one by Matthew. When I read them, I realized I had forgotten his wilderness experiences and his count it all joy training.

One reason we forget about Paul's life is that our own trials usually overshadow anything else. Let's look at Paul's count it all joy training in 2 Corinthians 11:22-31 ESV. It says it best:

> "Are they Hebrews? So am I. Are they Israelites? So am I. Are they offspring of Abraham? So am I. Are they servants of Christ? I am a better one–I am talking like a madman–with far greater labors, far more imprisonments, with countless beatings, and often near death. Five times I received at the hands of the Jews the forty lashes less one. Three times I was beaten with rods. Once I was stoned. Three times I was shipwrecked; a night and a day I was adrift at sea; on frequent journeys, in danger from rivers, danger from robbers, danger from my own people, danger from Gentiles, danger in the city, danger in the wilderness, danger at sea, danger from false brothers; in toil and hardship, through many a sleepless night, in hunger and thirst, often without food, in cold and exposure. And, apart from other things, there is the daily pressure on me of my anxiety for all the churches. Who is weak, and I am not weak? Who is made to fall, and I am not indignant? If I must boast, I will boast of the things that show my weakness. The God and Father of the Lord Jesus, he who is blessed forever, knows that I am not lying." 2 Corinthians 11:22-31 ESV

The things Paul lists here in this passage are more than minor inconveniences like many of us face. These are serious, life threatening, and mentally taxing events. It's real persecution; however, he learned to count it all joy. Do you think Paul never doubted? Of course He did. He was human, just like us.

I am sure thoughts like, "**God, are you really there?**" came to Paul. "**Have you abandoned me, God?**" "**Is my faith working?**"

He may have felt like me, "**What in the wilderness is going on?**" I know Paul had struggles and doubts just like us; however, the scripture clearly shows he had learned to count. In Philippians 3:8, he says;

> *"Yet indeed I also count all things loss for the excellence of the knowledge of Christ Jesus my Lord, for whom I have suffered the loss of all things, and count them as rubbish, that I may gain Christ," Philippians 3:8 NKJV*

THE LENS OF JOY

So how did James, the chief apostle, say count it all joy? The Lord spoke to me through a visit with my ophthalmologist. He showed me about the lens of joy! He impressed this in my heart; "**Intimacy with Me in your present trial produces the lens of joy to live an abundant life.**"

Let me give you a little back story. Every two years, I go to the eye doctor and we play what I call the lens game. The real name for the piece of equipment is a phoropter. It is an instrument fitted with various lenses you look through in order to determine your eyeglass prescription. It also helps identify if you are nearsighted, far-sighted or have astigmatism. It takes time to switch the various lenses as you look through them to get the optimum vision. The doctor adjusts the lenses, you look through them at the reading chart, and he asks, "Better here?" Then he flips the lens and asks, "Or here?" I must admit sometimes he flips the lens so much I just want to give up and say, "Whatever?" It's really quite amusing to me sometimes. On a side note; one time I told the doctor that I could just imagine everyone at the yearly Ophthalmology convention laughing about all the people you messed with just using one lens back and forth. He thought it was funny as well. In the end, the doctor gets me the right prescription so I can see clearly.

GOD is like the eye doctor. Every day, especially in the trial, various lenses are presented to us.

THREE TYPES OF LENSES.

God's Word is a lens. Our human reasoning is a lens, and the enemy has a lens. God's Word is the only true and clear lens. Our unrenewed minds and the enemy both present a skewed lens. Satan will bring fear and intimidation to get us to quit. He wants us depressed and hopeless. The enemy and our unrenewed mind will see everything that's against us. They magnify every situation until a molehill becomes a mountain. Fear, worry, discouragement and hopelessness all flash in front of our eyes. The lens goes from bad to worse. Worry goes south real fast. The worry doctor says, "**Is it worse here or here as He flips the lens?**"

THINGS JESUS NEVER SAID

One day I woke up and the first thing on my mind was this; Things Jesus never said: Jesus never said, I'm worried! That's almost ridiculous to imagine. Matthew records how futile worry is in our lives.

> *"Therefore I say to you, do not worry about your life, what you will eat or what you will drink; nor about your body, what you will put on. Is not life more than food and the body more than clothing? Look at the birds of the air, for they neither sow nor reap nor gather into barns; yet your heavenly Father feeds them. Are you not of more value than they? Which of you by worrying can add one cubit to his stature? "So why do you worry about clothing? Consider the lilies of the field, how they grow: they neither toil nor spin; and yet I say to you that even Solomon in all his glory was not [c]arrayed like one of these. Now if God so clothes the grass of the field, which today is, and tomorrow is thrown into the oven, will He not much more clothe you, O you of little faith? "Therefore do not worry, saying, 'What shall we eat?' or 'What shall we drink?' or 'What shall we wear?' For after all these things the Gentiles seek. For your heavenly Father knows that you need all these things. But seek first the kingdom of God and His righteousness, and all these things shall be*

added to you. Therefore do not worry about tomorrow, for tomorrow will worry about its own things. Sufficient for the day is its own trouble." Matthew 6:25-34 NKJV

Remember that feelings have no identity, they are led by thoughts. If you tell me what you are feeling, I can tell you what types of thoughts you have been thinking. We have been counting problems, not counting it all joy.

When Jesus, the great physician, comes in, He gets us tweaked so we can see clearly! Jesus is very much into our vision, and there is no better eye doctor anywhere. He says,

"Greater is He that's in you, than he that's in the world" 1 John 4:4 NKJV

JOY is the lens God gives His children. It's a gift and a weapon in our life. We must use it. We will not make it long term in our walk without JOY.

Nehemiah 8:10 states: "The joy of the lord is our strength!"

JOY PROVIDES A DIFFERENT "NOT STINKY" PERSPECTIVE

When we see through the lens of joy, it changes our entire perspective. One time my family and I were going to an apple festival in Burlington, WV. On the way we stopped at a scenic overlook above the Festival. It was beautiful. The sun shining on the mountains and the clear blue sky were breathtaking. We took some pictures and then climbed into the car and made our way down the mountain to the festival. Upon arrival I had to go to the porta potty to use the bathroom. I looked out the little screen window in back of the porta potty and noticed that I could look up and see the scenic overlook where we stood just minutes before. I realized at that moment that joy is about perspective. We can have a porta potty perspective that really stinks, or we can have God's perspective and see through the lens of joy. I will never see a porta potty or a scenic overlook the same again. They are reminders of learning to count. To make life count every day, we must learn to count God's way.

QUESTIONS TO CONSIDER

1. How has this chapter helped you to learn to count?

2. Is there an area of your life that you need to fully surrender to God and trust Him?

3. Do you count blessings or counting problems?

4. Do you have a porta potty perspective or God's perspective?

Chapter 11

STRENGTH IN THE SUFFERING

SUFFER

To feel or bear what is painful, disagreeable, either to the body or mind; to undergo. We suffer pain of the body; we suffer grief of the mind. The criminal suffers punishment; the sinner suffers the pangs of conscience in this life, and is condemned to suffer the wrath of an offended God. We often suffer wrong; we suffer abuse; we suffer injustice. * Noah Websters 1828 dictionary

Suffering is a missing subject in the Modern Church in America, but it's a reality for every Christian, for some more than others. Suffering has been like the elephant in the kitchen that no one wants to talk about, but it is part of the wilderness journey. I admit, as a young Christian, I had an unspoken belief that if I didn't talk about it, then it wouldn't happen. Then, as a faith-filled Christian, I had an unspoken belief that if I had enough faith, I would never suffer. I didn't hear messages about suffering, so I stayed away from it as well. Through my suffering and study, I realized it's an important topic and close to the heart of God.

In fact, 2 Timothy 2:12 states:

"If we suffer, we shall also reign with him: if we deny him, he also will deny us." 2 Timothy 2:12 KJV

IT COMES WITH THE TERRITORY

The idea of suffering here is enduring hardship, remaining true to Christ and not rejecting Him, no matter what. The contrast is when we reject and deny Christ because of hard circumstances. Honestly, I believe much of the modern gospel is creating fair weather believers when the true Gospel of Jesus Christ includes the truth about suffering. You could say suffering comes with territory of following Christ. We must arm ourselves with the mind of Christ and gear ourselves through intimacy with Him to endure whatever we may face in life. Tomorrow is a mystery, but we must realize He is already there. He has suffered more than any of us can imagine, yet He endured. He was accustomed to persecution, ridicule, mockery, betrayal and the horrific torment, torture, and death. The Good News is that He defeated death, hell and the grave for us, and He rose again to live now and forever! The same Spirit that raised Him from the dead is in us! I Praise Jesus that He didn't shrink from suffering and He paved the way for you and me to make it through anything in life.

God is faithful in suffering. I love what 1 Peter 4:1-2 states;

> *So, since Christ suffered in the flesh for us, for you, arm yourselves with the same thought and purpose [patiently to suffer rather than fail to please God]. For whoever has suffered in the flesh [having the mind of Christ] is done with [intentional] sin [has stopped pleasing himself and the world, and pleases God], 2 So that he can no longer spend the rest of his natural life living by [his] human appetites and desires, but [he lives] for what God wills. 1 Peter 4:1-2 AMPC*

Suffering is a product of the fall, a consequence of human sin against God (Romans 5:12; 1 Corinthians 15:21). Suffering is in our lives because we are living in a broken world. Some suffering is because of our sinful and wrong choices, but some are due simply to the world being a fallen world. We have all witnessed that bad things happen to good people.

1 Peter has a lot to say about endurance through seasons of unjust sufferings that Christians go through. When we look at the Heroes of Faith and how Christ Himself suffered,

it should be no surprise to us we will go through suffering ourselves.

When we don't preach and teach the Gospel of suffering, we do Jesus a disservice, and the gospel we preach is false or at least incomplete. We may even be part of people feeling frustrated at God during their season of suffering. I believe 100 percent in speaking life and not death over myself and others, but suffering is a reality.

SUFFERING IS TEMPORARY

During Peter's time with Jesus, he witnessed firsthand the sufferings his Lord went through. Later in his life he faced suffering himself, but realized Christ is truly our Hope! God wants to arm us with what we need in our own season of suffering just like He did for Peter.

Peter states:

> "And the God of all grace, who called you to his eternal glory in Christ, after you have suffered a little while, will himself restore you and make you strong and steadfast." 1 Peter 5:10 NKJV

I love the insight from this verse. He says after you have suffered a little while. "Suffering a little" while implies two things;

1. Suffering is a season, not a lifetime. Any suffering we go through has a time limit and an expiration date.

2. Suffering in this life is not long compared to the glorious eternity we will spend with Him.

Then Peter says that suffering has an outcome. Christ Himself will come and restore us, make us strong, make us firm and make us steadfast. This is such a life-changing promise. The One who suffered most is the One who comes to our aid in suffering. This is a promise I revisit again and again.

IT'S A PACKAGE DEAL

We have made suffering "Taboo" in the church. We have failed to understand that to truly understand resurrection, we must understand suffering, death, burial, and resurrection as a package. That's the beauty of the Gospel. Everyone deals with suffering in life, so we must address it. Some try to dress it up, put makeup on it, put a mask on it, and try to hide it. Others try to busy it up, drink it up, party it up, or sweep it under the rug. In reality, we must face it. I always say, "**We must face it because it is facing us**."

HE IS WITH ME

Sometimes, especially when you are a parent or a leader, you are forced to have private moments of suffering in front of everyone. I had to do this as a husband, father, and minister.

One time, when I was in the ICU for twenty-one days

after my appendix burst, I had a real hard moment. A person came to see me in the hospital, and I know they meant well, but they carried me an evil report. They came to my bedside and said, "**Do you know what they are saying about you?**"

I said, "**No**." Then they said, "**They are saying, that man of faith, where is His God now?**" I know in that moment the Lord gave me the words to say, because the words He said cut into my heart. I said, "**God is in the same place He was when His son Jesus was dying on the cross.**" "**He is with me.**" I had to face it, because it was facing me. God gave me the victory in my suffering. God brought me through, and He will bring you through as well.

WE ALL SUFFER

Remember that when you suffer, those who love you most also suffer in their own way. I never realized, until I came out of this last battle I had, how hard it was on my wife and family, especially my youngest daughter, Anna. I could only see what I was facing, but they were facing a life without me and dealing with their own suffering, fears, and questions.

The fact is that we all suffer. Male and female suffer. Young and old suffer. Every race, tribe, tongue and nationality suffer.

I worked in a bar before I was a Christian. We had what I call "Barology", which is Bar Room Theology. It usually happened around 4am when people were still trying to drink their problems away. Someone would say, "**So and so was born with a silver spoon in their mouth. If I was like that, my life would be good**." In reality, money can't buy us out of suffering. Suffering happens to us all. The only one we can trust for advice is the only one who suffered and died for us all. His name is Jesus.

He is faithful in suffering. Paul states,

> *"Being confident of this very thing, that He who has begun a good work in you will complete it until the day of Jesus Christ." Philippians 1:6 NKJV*

The other day I wrote in my journal; "**When you are pregnant with purpose, let nothing abort the process**". The process is necessary. Let nothing within or without abort the process, even when that process includes suffering.

THE PRESSURE TEST

I have learned in the past three decades that every prophetic promise gets pressure tested like steel.

The point of breaking becomes the point where God will strengthen us to continue in His strength. Going from Glory to Glory is not floating on a cloud, but walking through the God process in our life. Remember that what you may go through now will enable you to overcome the next step and move on! He who began a good work in you will complete it.

Stay humble, faithful, and thankful when you are suffering in the middle of the process

HOW TO BE UNSTOPPABLE IN SUFFERING

Therefore submit to God. Resist the devil and he will flee from you. Draw near to God and He will draw near to you. Cleanse your hands, you sinners; and purify your hearts, you double-minded." James 4:7-8 NKJV

When we submit to God and walk in obedience to Him and His Word and then resist the devil, he has to flee. He has to run the other direction because God's Word is true! God will vindicate you, and God will exalt you at just the right time. When we do both parts of this verse, we become unstoppable.

Never think you are crazy about going through suffering. Again we look at First Peter.

"Dear friends, don't be surprised at the fiery trials you are going through, as if something strange were happening to you. Instead, be very glad–for these trials make you partners with Christ in his suffering, so that you will have the wonderful joy of seeing his glory when it is revealed to all the world. If you are insulted because you bear the name of Christ, you will be blessed, for the glorious Spirit of God rests upon you. If you suffer, however, it must not be for murder, stealing, making trouble, or

prying into other people's affairs. But it is no shame to suffer for being a Christian. Praise God for the privilege of being called by his name! For the time has come for judgment, and it must begin with God's household. And if judgment begins with us, what terrible fate awaits those who have never obeyed God's Good News? And also, "If the righteous are barely saved, what will happen to godless sinners?" So if you are suffering in a manner that pleases God, keep on doing what is right, and trust your lives with the God who created you, for he will never fail you. 1 Peter 4:12-19 NLT

God is faithful! He Himself will restore you and make you strong, firm, and steadfast. This is a fabulous promise. Fiery trails make Golden Christians. Suffering brought the early church together. I heard a great general in the Faith, Dr. John Kelly, say one time, "**Covenant relationships are forged in foxholes, not times of ease.**" When I see how suffering touched the church throughout the ages, I can see that statement is true. Suffering has always caused the Gospel to spread, and it's no different today.

GOD ISN'T WONDERING HOW YOU MIGHT MAKE IT THROUGH YOUR TIME OF SUFFERING IN THE WILDERNESS. HE HAS THE PERFECT PLAN. WE MUST TRUST HIM TO SEE US THROUGH!

Paul states in 2 Corinthians;

"For we walk by faith, not by sight." 2 Corinthians 5:7 NKJV

I challenge you today to stand up wherever you are and choose to trust God, no matter what it looks like. Choose to believe Him who is invisible. Take this book as a personal prophecy in your wilderness. Submit to God, resist the devil, and he has to flee. What God started in you, He will complete.

I pray this will help you in any season of suffering you will ever walk through and may you use what you learned to help others.

QUESTIONS TO CONSIDER

1. As you reflect on a past season of suffering or a season of suffering you may be in presently, how has this chapter helped you to be better prepared for the future?

2. Are you currently obeying both parts of James 4:7-8 by submitting to God and resisting the devil?

3. Would you say you are living by faith or sight?

4. What areas do you need to study in God's Word to help you better arm yourself with the mind of Christ? By being faithful, humble or thankful?

Chapter 12

A ROAD IN YOUR WILDERNESS AND RIVERS IN YOUR DESSERT

FOLLOW THE OLD RIVER ROAD

When I was a little boy, I attended a small church called Selbysport United Methodist. I have many fond memories of these simpler times from my childhood. The people, the ice cream socials, the Christmas Eve services and the friends we made there. Several people from that era had a great impact on my life, not to mention that John Wesley is one of my heroes of the faith. This little Methodist church was several miles from my home, and right at the entrance of the Youghiogheny River and the Youghiogheny Lake. As a kid, we rode dirt bikes in the summer and snowmobiles in the winter down the old river road. I vividly remember riding down that road for the first time alone. My mom's instructions to me were as follows, **"If you break down, or something happens, just follow the old river road home. I will look for you there."**

I sense the Lord saying the same thing to you today on your journey through the wilderness.

His Word says, in Isaiah 43:19;

> *"Behold, I will do a new thing, now it shall spring forth; shall you not know it? I will even make a road in the wilderness and rivers in the desert. God will make a road in your wilderness and rivers in your dessert." Isaiah 43:19 NKJV*

God always makes a way through the wilderness, even when there seems to be no way we will make it. I have a verse from Job 28:7 which has always given me hope to stand on. It states;

> *"There is a path which no fowl knoweth, and which the vulture's eye hath not seen." Job 28:7 KJV*

We realize God is a Creator, and Satan is a counterfeiter. God has ways to create a road in the wilderness and rivers in the dessert that no other created being has a clue about.

God can even make a tunnel through the mountain if need be.

GOD NOT ONLY HAS A PLAN FOR YOUR LIFE, HE HAS A PATH FOR YOU TO WALK ON TO COMPLETE THE PLAN.

Even when we stray or get off the path, He has a way of making roads when we will follow and be obedient to Him. When I read this verse, it makes me think of how He can cover us and camouflage us from the enemy. We walk in the wilderness and God hides us from the enemy's eyes. That vulture thinks he has us defeated and then, on the other side of the mountain, we appear. On the other side of the wilderness, we are alive and well. On the other side of death, we are resurrected, just like Jesus.

The last two chapters in this book were parallels in my life. I went through a season of suffering and then I found myself on a new road. It was a new road where God was doing a new thing for a new season. I found myself in the River.

Psalm 46:4 says,

> *"There is a river whose streams shall make glad the city of God, The holy place of the tabernacle of the Most High."*
> *Psalm 46:4 NKJV*

The river of God in our life is as vital to our walk with God as water is to our human existence. No one can survive long without water, and it's important we find water in the wilderness.

Psalm 42:1 says,

"As the deer pants for streams of water, so my soul pants
for you, O God. My soul thirst for God, for the living God.
Where can I go and meet with God?" Psalm 42:1 NKJV

This longing for living water is something God will always fill. He says in Matthew 5 that if we hunger and thirst for righteousness, we will be filled.

The prophet Ezekiel gives us a special insight into the River of God in Ezekiel 47:1-12. Let's start with verses 1-2;

"Then he brought me back to the door of the temple; and
there was water flowing from under the threshold of the
temple toward the east, for the front of the temple faced
east; the water was flowing from under the right side of
the temple, south of the altar. He brought me out by way
of the north gate and led me around on the outside to
the outer gateway that faces east; and there was water
running out on the right side." Ezekiel 47:1-2 NKJV

The prophet Ezekiel shows us here that we must find the source of the river. When we find the source of the river in the wilderness, we will never have to be concerned about making it through the wilderness. The door here points to Jesus. To have revival in our lives, our churches, or our nation, it will always bring us back to the source and the door, which is Jesus.

Our door is our heart. Jesus constantly comes to the door of our heart and knocks. He doesn't just knock at salvation; He knocks frequently when we are shutting Him out. If you are in the condition today where you have shut Him out or never opened to Him, then He is knocking on the door of your temple. I pray you will have ears to hear and eyes to see what he is saying to you through this book. Then I pray you would have the wisdom to open the door of your heart to Him in total surrender.

Revelation 3:20 Jesus states;

> *"Behold, I stand at the door and knock. If anyone hears my voice and opens the door, I will come in to him and eat with him, and he with me." Revelation 3:20 NKJV*

When we open up to Jesus and totally surrender, it's like getting totally immersed in the river of God. When we look at Ezekiels's word in Chapter 47, we clearly see that the river doesn't come from the White House, a King's Palace, a dictator's throne, a sport's stadium or anywhere else. The river in the wilderness comes from God.

Ezekiel 47:3 states

> *"And when the man went out to the east with the line in his hand, he measured one thousand cubits, and he*

brought me through the waters; the water came up to my ankles." Ezekiel 47:3 NKJV

Walking in the Spirit means we are led by The Holy Spirit even in the wilderness. Jesus was led by The Holy Spirit into the wilderness, but the good news is He was also led out of the wilderness and not just left there. The Holy Spirit will do the same for us.

JUMP IN THE RIVER

God doesn't just want us to look at the river, He wants us to get in and experience the river. The same is true of the Bible. God doesn't just want us to read the Bible, but He wants us to experience it!

Ezekiel 47:4 states;

> *Again, he measured one thousand and brought me through the waters; the water came up to my knees. Again, he measured one thousand and brought me through; the water came up to my waist. Ezekiel 47:4 NKJV*

God takes us through the river from the ankles, to the knees, to the waist. This principal is one of spiritual growth and maturity. Our walk with God takes us through progressive spiritual growth. The truth of God's Word makes us free. The more truth we get and apply is relative to our progressive growth. In turn, we experience more freedom, more renewing of our mind. We will continue until we are transformed into the image of Christ in all facets. 2 Corinthians 3:18.

I love the saying I heard years ago, which states; "**I am saved, I am being saved and I will be saved.**" - Unknown

This saying sums up the progression God takes us through as we walk with Him.

Then back to Ezekiel 47:5

> *"Again he measured one thousand, and it was a river that I could not cross; for the water was too deep, water in which one must swim, a river that could not be crossed." Ezekiel 47:5 NKJV*

Verse five is a place of total trust in God. We are no longer in control and must fully trust God. Our feet can not touch bottom. Fear is broken, anxiety is broken and worry has to come off. It's like the line from the movie "Nemo." "**Just keep swimming**". We just keep swimming and God does the rest. Don't stop, just keep going.

Let's finish reading Ezekiel 47:6-12;

> *"He said to me, "Son of man, have you seen this?" Then he brought me and returned me to the bank of the river. When I returned, there, along the bank of the river, were very many trees on one side and on the other. Then he said to me: "This water flows toward the eastern*

region, goes down into the valley, and enters the sea. When it reaches the sea, its waters are healed. And it shall be that every living thing that moves, wherever the rivers go, will live. There will be a very great multitude of fish, because these waters go there; for they will be healed, and everything will live wherever the river goes. It shall be that fishermen will stand by it from En Gedi to En Eglaim; they will be places for spreading their nets. Their fish will be of the same kinds as the fish of the Great Sea, exceedingly many. But its swamps and marshes will not be healed; they will be given over to salt. Along the bank of the river, on this side and that, will grow all kinds of trees used for food; their leaves will not wither, and their fruit will not fail. They will bear fruit every month, because their water flows from the sanctuary. Their fruit will be for food, and their leaves for medicine." Ezekiel 47:6-12 NKJV

This is just so good. It ties everything together in this survival guide in the wilderness. The words God gives us on being like a tree, and the truths in His Word about trees all come to play here. We see a beautiful picture of trees planted on both sides of the river. We are the trees of strength planted by the rivers of living water. This is liberating in the wilderness. God gives us a river in the wilderness that is fully accessible as we progressively grow up into Christ. The river flows from the source or mouth of God and it goes down into the valley.

The Lord spoke to my heart; "**The oldest rivers are found in the valleys they have cut.**"

THERE IS AN UNENDING SUPPLY OF NUTRIENTS FOR YOU WHEN YOU FIND YOURSELF IN THE WILDERNESS VALLEY.

All the nutrients that come from the mountain flow into the valley. There is a river of strength that can only be accessed by going through the wilderness valley. Our access point is Jesus. He is the way, the truth, the life and the door. He is not only the Lilly in the valley; He is the source of living water. If you find yourself in the wilderness valley today, there is a river of God's hope, healing and strength for you!

Revelation 22:1-5 states a beautiful promise;

"And he showed me a pure river of water of life, clear as crystal, proceeding from the throne of God and of the Lamb. In the middle of its street, and on either side of the river, was the tree of life, which bore twelve fruits, each tree yielding its fruit every month. The leaves of the tree were for the healing of the nations. And there shall be no more curse, but the throne of God and of the Lamb shall be in it, and His servants shall serve Him. They shall see His face, and His name shall be on their foreheads. There shall be no night there: They need no lamp nor light of the sun, for the Lord God gives them light. And they shall reign forever and ever." Revelation 22:1-5 NKJV

Then the Apostle John says;

*On the last day, that great day of the feast, Jesus stood
and cried out, saying, "If anyone thirsts, let him come to
Me and drink. He who believes in Me, as the Scripture
has said, out of his heart will flow rivers of living water."
John 7:37-38 NKJV*

Years ago, our theme for Fire in the Mountains/FireBrand
was "Voices Crying in the Wilderness." This book is a voice
crying in the wilderness.

John states;

*"Then they said to him,"Who are you, that we may give
an answer to those who sent us? What do you say about
yourself?" He said: "I am The voice of one crying in the
wilderness: "Make straight the way of the Lord," as the
prophet Isaiah said." John 1:22-23 NKJV*

I believe God is raising up people all over the world from
the wilderness to prepare the way of the Lord. I believe you
are one of those people, just like me. You are a voice from
the wilderness that will prepare the way of the Lord! The
wilderness you have experienced will be the proving ground
for the message God has placed within you. When it's all
said and done, your voice will make an eternal difference.

I want to leave you with this from my journal;

*Go and keep going! Go into all the world may
sound exciting to some and scary to others.*

Go into all the world may mean going to many nations in your lifetime or going a few miles outside your door to the same job, the same small business or the same small town church. The important thing to God is that we are willing to GO and keep going.

God loves it when we are faithful to just go every day.

One day we will cross heaven's shores and it will be worth it after all. When we hear the words, "Well Done!" Keep going because that next one you share Christ with has been waiting their whole life to hear the truth you hold within you!

You are a voice crying in the Wilderness!

Go today friends, not because you feel like it, but because you have to. It's your purpose!

Just keep going, it makes an eternal difference....
Mike Robinson

QUESTIONS TO CONSIDER

1. Have you totally surrendered to Jesus today? If so, how has it changed your life?

2. Are there any areas you must give up control in order to get into the deep water? If so, what are they?

3. What is the hardest part about giving up control?

4. How has this chapter helped you identify the river in the wilderness?

5. Are you willing to be a voice crying in the wilderness?

About The Author

Mike Robinson was radically saved in 1989. He and his wife Sandy began Pastoring only a year later in 1990 in their hometown where they still reside. They planted the church where they still pastor today, Anchor Church, in 1995. They have a strong emphasis on prayer, evangelism, discipleship and reaching every generation. In 2005, Mike wrote a book titled, Somebody Has to Wear the Shoes, about passing the baton of ministry to the next generation. He founded Firebrand in 2007, which has become a revival movement that reaches the next generation.

He and his wife are foodies and run a cafe. They love hosting their friends and family. One of his favorite pastimes is sharing life stories, while enjoying a good laugh. Mike spends his spare time studying the Bible, revival and the hero's of the faith. He also enjoys looking at vintage vehicles, taking a drive in the country, and stopping at a thrift store or yard sale.

Mike's life is marked by his love for God, his family, and people from all walks of life. He has a passion to see people anchored in Jesus and desires to equip people to withstand any storm! He also hosts "Anchored with Mike Robinson" a weekly podcast and radio program.

www.ingramcontent.com/pod-product-compliance
Lightning Source LLC
Chambersburg PA
CBHW072348090426
42741CB00012B/2977